# ENGLISH SPOKEN HERE

## Health and Safety

Jerry L. Messec
Roger E. Kranich

**CAMBRIDGE**
THE ADULT EDUCATION COMPANY
New York • Toronto

**Executive Editor:** Brian Schenk
**Project Editor:** Eva Holzer
**Project Consultants:** Laurel T. Ellis
Don Williams

Copyright © 1982 by Cambridge Book Company. **All rights reserved.**
No part of this work covered by the copyrights hereon may be reproduced or used in any form or by any means—graphic, electronic, or mechanical, including photocopying, recording, or information storage and retrieval systems—without the written permission of the publisher. Manufactured in the United States of America.

ISBN: 0-8428-0852-3

9 8 7 6 5 4 3

# CONTENTS

Unit 1.  How Are You Feeling?           iv

Unit 2.  What Did the Doctor Say?       34

Unit 3.  Which Medicine Should I Take?  66

Unit 4.  This Is an Emergency!          96

Unit 5.  Is That Good for You?          126

# UNIT 1

## HOW ARE YOU FEELING?

IN THIS UNIT YOU WILL LEARN:

the names of parts of the body
the names of common aches,
    pains, and illnesses
how to describe the location
    of pain and how it feels
how to ask about a person's health
how to show sympathy
how to give advice

As you go through this unit,
    notice the following:

**be** + the past participle (the passive voice)
**should, ought to,** and **had better**
**'s** to show possession
adjectives (words that describe)
intensifiers and qualifiers (words to use
    with adjectives)
verb forms used as adjectives

**LOOK AT THE PICTURE.**
Find these things in the picture.

1. patients
2. waiting room
3. receptionist
4. doctor/physician
5. cast
6. x-ray room
7. crutches
8. examining room
9. examining table
10. (neck) brace

1

# TALK TOPICS

**LOOK AT THE PICTURES.
Talk about what you see.**

What is this place?
Why are these people here?
What parts of their bodies have
    they injured?
Describe their injuries.

What is the x-ray room?
How does a doctor know if a bone
    is broken?
How does a doctor know when a bone
    is healed?

Talk about your experiences at a
    doctor's office.

Have you been injured?   How?
What part of your body was injured?
Did you need a cast?   a bandage?
    a brace?

What are some differences between
    this picture and the first one?
Talk about what has changed.

**ASK ABOUT OTHER THINGS IN THE PICTURE.**
Use these question words: who, what, where, when, which, how.
Write your new words.

11. _____   16. _____
12. _____   17. _____
13. _____   18. _____
14. _____   19. _____
15. _____   20. _____

3

# NAMING PARTS OF THE BODY

**LOOK AT THESE PICTURES.**
Name the body parts.
Write the names of the body parts next to the numbers.
Use the words in the list on the next page.

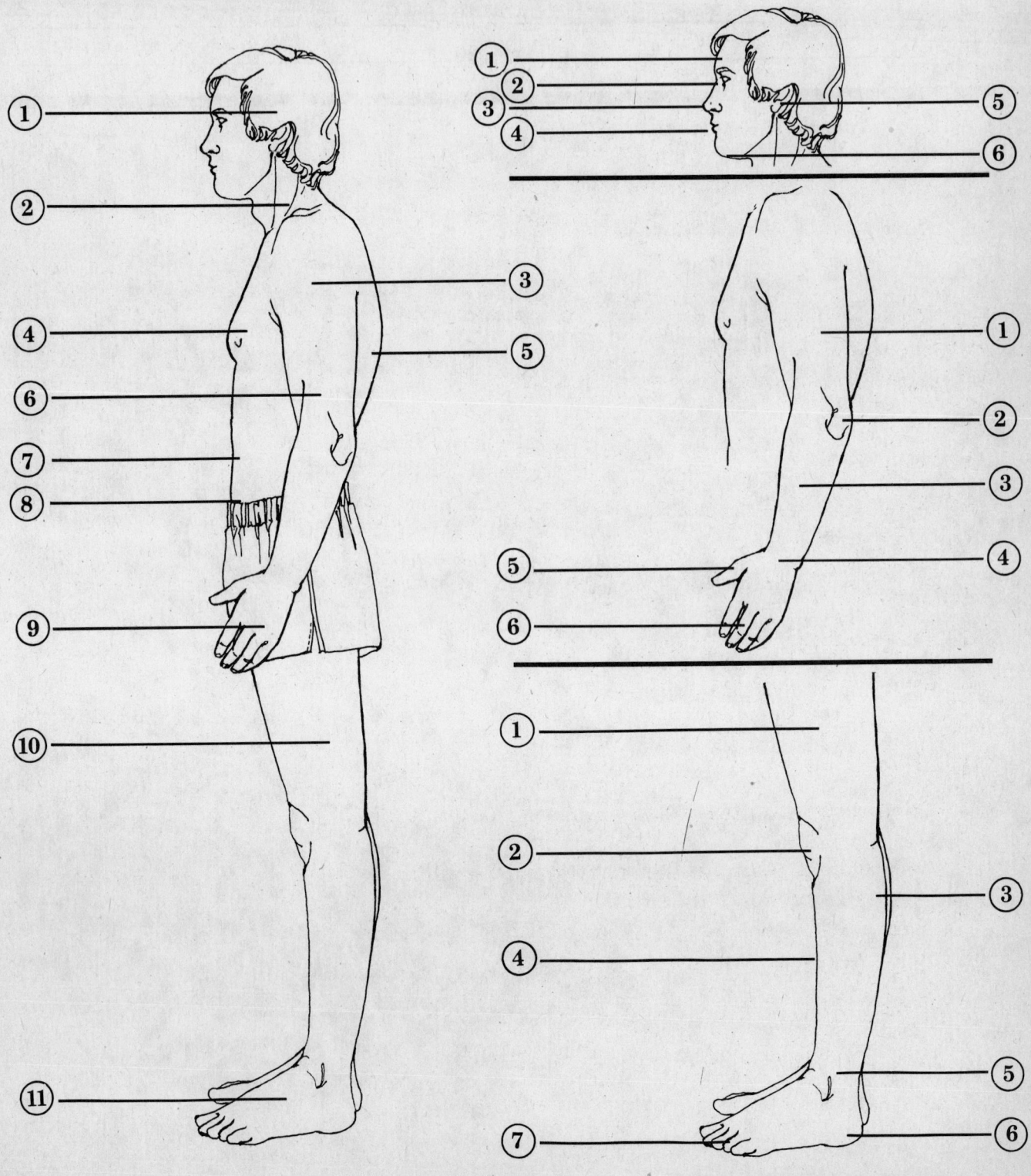

**TRY IT IN CLASS.**
**Practice describing pain.**
**Write sentences.**

A. Carla/stiff/shoulder
   Carla has a stiff shoulder.   OR   Carla's shoulder is stiff.

B. My/feet/very/sore

C. I/dull/ache/my/tooth

D. Mike/throbbing/pain/ear

E. She/bad/headache

F. It/burning/feeling

G. Your/leg/achy/stiff

H. You/bad/stomachache?


**TRY IT IN CLASS.**
**One student has a pain.   The other asks questions about it.**

    YOU:  Ask how the person feels.
PERSON:  Tell about your sore arm.
    YOU:  Ask where it hurts.
PERSON:  Tell about your elbow.
    YOU:  Ask what kind of pain it is.
PERSON:  Describe the pain.
    YOU:  Ask if person can bend elbow.
PERSON:  Say how you can move it.

# ASKING ABOUT HEALTH/SHOWING SYMPATHY

**LISTEN TO THESE PEOPLE.**
They are talking about how they feel.

How are you feeling?
I feel kind of sick.
I'm sorry to hear that. What's the matter?
My arms and legs ache.

I'm not feeling well.
That's too bad. What's wrong?
I've got a headache. My head hurts a lot.
Do you have a stomachache, too?
Yes, it's really bothering me.
Sounds like the flu. I hope you feel better soon.

What's the matter with your eye?
I have something in it.
Let me help you get it out.
Thanks.

You look sick. Are you all right?
I'm fine. I'm just a little tired.

**FILL IN THE MISSING WORDS.**
**Practice talking about how people feel.**

A. How _____ you feeling?

  I _____ kind of sick.

  _____ to hear that. What's the _____ ?

  I have a cold. I'm _____ a temperature.

B. You look sick. Are you _____ right?

  I'm fine. I'm just a _____ tired.

C. What's the _____ with your leg?

  It's nothing. It's a _____ stiff.

D. My sister broke her arm.

  I'm _____ to hear that. How _____ it happen?

  She fell _____ the stairs.

  Tell her I _____ she feels better.

E. _____ you feel OK? You look _____ you're in pain.

  It's _____ . My stomach's kind _____ sore.

15

**TRY IT IN CLASS.**
**Practice asking people how they feel.**
**Practice giving sympathy.**

A. YOU: _____ (how feeling?)
PERSON: _____ (feel sick)
YOU: _____ (matter?)
PERSON: _____ (headache)
YOU: _____ (feel like?)
PERSON: _____ (sharp)
YOU: _____ (where?)
PERSON: _____ (above right eye)
YOU: _____ (sorry; better soon)

B. YOU: _____ (feel OK?)
PERSON: _____ (stomachache)
YOU: _____ (sore throat too?)
PERSON: _____ (yes; feel hot)
YOU: _____ (may be flu; feel better)

C. YOU: _____ (happened?)
PERSON: _____ (sprained ankle)
YOU: _____ (how?)
PERSON: _____ (fell on ice)
YOU: _____ (lucky only a sprain).

D. PERSON: _____ (sore neck)
YOU: _____ (stiff?)
PERSON: _____ (a little)
YOU: _____ (where?)
PERSON: _____ (left side)
YOU: _____ (near shoulder?)
PERSON: _____ (closer to ear)
YOU: _____ (feel better soon)

**E.** YOU: _____ (happened?)

PERSON: _____ (broke arm)

YOU: _____ (how?)

PERSON: _____ (fell down stairs)

YOU: _____ (sorry; which arm?)

PERSON: _____ (right)

**F.** YOU: _____ (all right?)

PERSON: _____ (little tired)

**G.** YOU: _____ (matter with eye?)

PERSON: _____ (dust in it)

YOU: _____ (help get out)

PERSON: _____ (thanks)

**H.** PERSON: _____ (not feeling well)

YOU: _____ (too bad; wrong?)

PERSON: _____ (have cold)

YOU: _____ (temperature?)

PERSON: _____ (a little feverish)

YOU: _____ (sore throat?)

PERSON: _____ (little; stuffy nose)

YOU: _____ (feel better)

**J.** PERSON: _____ (burned finger)

YOU: _____ (how?)

PERSON: _____ (hot tea kettle)

# GIVING ADVICE

**LISTEN TO THESE PEOPLE.**
**One person is talking about an injury.**
**The other person is giving advice.**

I bumped my head. Now I have a bump on my forehead.

You ought to put some ice on it.

I burned my finger.

You had better run some cold water on it.

I've cut my hand. It's bleeding.

You should put a bandage on it.

My ears and my throat are killing me.

Sounds pretty bad. Why don't you call the doctor. Tell him you have an earache and a sore throat.

That's a good idea.

I think I've sprained my ankle.

Can you walk?

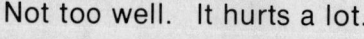
Not too well. It hurts a lot.

You ought to have it x-rayed. It may be broken.

18

**FILL IN THE MISSING WORDS.**
**Practice talking about injuries and giving advice.**

A. I've cut _____ foot. _____ bleeding.

　　You _____ to put a _____ on it.

B. Are _____ all right?

　　No. I bumped my knee. It _____ a lot.

　You had _____ put some ice _____ it.

C. I _____ I've sprained my ankle.

　　Can you _____ ?

　Not too _____ . It's _____ me.

　　You _____ have it _____ .

D. _____ wrong?

　　I burned _____ hand.

　You _____ better _____ some cold water on it.

　　_____ a good _____ .

E. _____ back is killing me!

　　Sounds pretty bad. _____ don't you _____ the doctor.

　　_____ him you have a bad _____ .

**TALK TO THESE PEOPLE.**
**Give them advice. Use <u>should</u>, <u>ought to</u>, or <u>had better</u>.**

A. PERSON: I've cut my toe.

B. PERSON: I think my arm is broken.

C. PERSON: My throat's sore and I feel hot.
　　　　　　What should I do?

D. PERSON: I burned my finger.

E. PERSON: I've bumped my knee. It's black and blue.

# ILLNESSES AND SYMPTOMS

**LOOK AT THIS CHART.**
It lists some common illnesses and their symptoms.
Read the chart in class. Talk about the illnesses you've had.

| ILLNESS | SYMPTOMS |
| --- | --- |
| allergy—reaction to certain foods, chemicals, or plants | skin rash; difficulty in breathing; teary eyes; sneezing; upset stomach or vomiting |
| appendicitis—infection of the appendix (in the lower part of the abdomen, below the stomach) | pain in the abdomen; vomiting; fever |
| chickenpox—usually a childhood disease—it is caused by a virus and is very contagious (spreads easily from one person to another) | itchy, red spots (blisters) over the chest, stomach, and back that become larger, open, and form a crust (scab) |
| cold (common cold)—infection of the upper chest | stuffy nose; fever; body aches; coughing; sneezing |
| flu (influenza)—infection of the upper chest caused by a virus; it is very contagious | fever; muscle aches and pains; headache; stuffy nose; sore throat; tiredness |
| heart attack—the clogging of an artery (passage) in the heart | pain in the upper left part of the chest and weakness in the left arm |
| measles—usually a childhood disease—it is caused by a virus and is very contagious | a rash that starts on the face and spreads to the rest of the body; fever; runny nose |
| mumps—a contagious childhood disease caused by a virus | swollen salivary glands (the top part of the neck and the lower part of the face); fever; pain in chewing and swallowing |
| tonsillitis—swelling of the tonsils (in the throat) | a sore, red throat; difficulty in swallowing; fever |

**LOOK AT THE CHART ON PAGE 20.**
**Answer the questions.**

A. What are some symptoms of a heart attack?
_____

B. What causes measles?
_____

C. What does "contagious" mean?
_____

D. What are some symptoms of appendicitis?
_____

E. What three childhood diseases are on the chart?
_____

F. What causes the flu?
_____

G. In what part of the body are the tonsils?
_____

H. What are some symptoms of the mumps?
_____

I. What is an allergy?
_____

J. In what part of the body is the appendix?
_____

K. What do these words mean?
   (1) reaction     (5) scab
   (2) rash        (6) artery
   (3) vomiting     (7) weakness
   (4) infection    (8) salivary glands

**LISTEN TO THESE PEOPLE.**
**They are describing symptoms to a doctor.**

My daughter has itchy red spots on her chest and back.

Did you take her temperature?

Yes, but she doesn't have a fever.

Sounds like the chickenpox. It's going around.

What should I do?

Keep her at home for a few days. Chickenpox is very contagious. Try to keep her from scratching.

What will happen if she scratches?

The sores can get infected and leave marks on her body.

Do you think I ought to give her some medicine?

No. If the itching is very bad, call me.

---

My wife feels very sick.

What's the matter with her?

She has a very sharp pain in her abdomen on the right side.

Did you take her temperature?

Yes. It's high. She has a fever.

Has she vomited?

Yes, a few times. What do you think is the problem?

It could be appendicitis. You had better take her to the hospital.

22

**FILL IN THE MISSING WORDS.**
**Practice describing symptoms and asking for advice.**

A.  My son doesn't feel _____ .
    What's the _____ with him?
He has a very _____ throat and can hardly swallow.
    Did you _____ his temperature?
Yes, it's high.  He has a _____ .
What do you _____ is the problem?
    It could _____ tonsillitis or only a cold.
    You had _____ bring him to my office.

B.  My muscles really _____ and I _____ a sore throat.
_____ you think I have the flu?
    Sounds like it.  It's _____ around.
Do you think I ought _____ take my temperature?
    Yes.  You may have a _____ .
_____ I take some medicine?
    You can _____ some aspirin.  You _____ better stay in bed.
What else _____ I do?
    You _____ drink a lot of juice and try to stay warm.

C.  My daughter's face _____ very swollen.
    Did _____ take _____ temperature?
No.  But _____ feels hot.
    Is _____ else bothering her?
It _____ when she swallows.  _____ do you think the problem is?
    Sounds _____ the mumps.
_____ you think I _____ keep her at _____ for a few days?
    Yes.  It _____ very contagious.

**LISTEN TO THESE PEOPLE.**
**The doctor is examining the patients and asking questions.**

**TALK TO THESE PEOPLE.**
**You are a patient.**
**Practice answering a doctor's questions.**

DOCTOR: What's the problem?
YOU: _____ (bad backache)

DOCTOR: Can you lie down?
YOU: _____ (yes, really stiff)

DOCTOR: Let's have a look at it. Where does it hurt?
YOU: _____ (below shoulders)

DOCTOR: Right here?
YOU: _____ (yes, very sore)

DOCTOR: I think you strained the muscles in your back.
You'll have to rest for a few days.
YOU: _____ (need medicine?)

DOCTOR: No. Just put a heating pad on your muscles.
You'll feel much better.

---

DOCTOR: What happened to you?
YOU: _____ (twisted foot)

DOCTOR: Where does it hurt?
YOU: _____ (below ankle)

DOCTOR: Let's have a look at it. Is the pain here?
YOU: _____ (yes, pretty sore)

DOCTOR: It looks like you have a sprained ankle.
I'll wrap a bandage around it.
YOU: _____ (bandage hurt?)

DOCTOR: No. Your ankle will feel much better.

# CLOSE-UP ON LANGUAGE

## Verb forms

Verbs have three basic forms: present, past, and past participle.
Look at the three forms of some verbs:

| VERB | PRESENT | PAST | PAST PARTICIPLE |
|---|---|---|---|
| Regular | | | |
| to bruise | bruise/bruises | bruised | bruised |
| to burn | burn/burns | burned | burned |
| to injure | injure/injures | injured | injured |
| to scrape | scrape/scrapes | scraped | scraped |
| to scratch | scratch/scratches | scratched | scratched |
| Irregular | | | |
| to be | am/is/are | was/were | been |
| to break | break/breaks | broke | broken |
| to cut | cut/cuts | cut | cut |
| to do | do/does | did | done |
| to eat | eat/eats | ate | eaten |
| to hurt | hurt/hurts | hurt | hurt |
| to make | make/makes | made | made |
| to pay | pay/pays | paid | paid |
| to read | read/reads | read | read |
| to write | write/writes | wrote | written |

The past participle is used with <u>has</u> or <u>have</u> in the present perfect tense.
(See "English Spoken Here: Consumer Information," unit 4 for a review of this tense.)

    I have <u>broken</u> my leg.    We have <u>opened</u> the door.
    He has <u>injured</u> his foot.    They have <u>made</u> an appointment.

The past participle is also used with <u>be</u> (passive voice sentences).

    My leg is <u>broken</u>.    My work is <u>done</u>.
    His foot is <u>injured</u>.    His finger is <u>cut</u>.

**WRITE NEW SENTENCES.**
**Use <u>be</u> + the past participle. That is, practice using the passive voice.**

  A.  I burned my hand.
                   My hand is burned.

**B.** She bruised her knee.
_____

**C.** Ellen paid her bill.
_____

**D.** He hurt his elbow.
_____

**E.** He cut his finger.
_____

**F.** She injured her ankle.
_____

**G.** The teacher wrote her name on the board.
_____

**H.** You hurt your elbow.
_____

**I.** I broke my arm.
_____

**J.** She wrote her name in the book.
_____

**K.** He sprained his wrist.
_____

**L.** She bandaged her toe.
_____

**M.** We did our work.
_____

**N.** Angela broke the dish.
_____

## Using should, ought to, and had better

Should, ought to, and had better are used to give advice:

    You should put a bandage on that cut.
    She ought to see a doctor.
    He had better lie down.

**WRITE NEW SENTENCES.**
**Use should, ought to, and had better.**

**A.** You/take/temperature
    You (should, ought to, had better) take your temperature.

**B.** She/go/hospital

**C.** He/go/bed

**D.** You/put/ice/on/bump

**E.** They/be/careful

**F.** She/get/foot/x-rayed

**G.** He/stop/smoking

**H.** You/take/hot/bath

**I.** They/stay/home

**J.** She/take/aspirin

**K.** You/use/heating pad

## Adding 's to singular nouns to show possession

Add 's to nouns to show possession.　　Don't add 's to pronouns.

POSSESSIVE NOUNS　　　　　　　　POSSESSIVE PRONOUNS

The doctor's office is closed.　　　　　His office is closed.
Marta's throat is sore.　　　　　　　　Her throat is sore.
Is Kim's arm broken?　　　　　　　　Yes, her arm is broken.

**FILL IN THE MISSING WORDS.**
**Add 's where it is needed.**

A. ____Sara's____ hand is burned. (Sara)
B. _____ finished his work. (Peter)
C. _____ shoulder is injured. (Tran)
D. _____ washed her clothes. (Yoko)
E. Isn't this book _____? (his)
F. That _____ briefcase was stolen. (man)
G. _____ broken leg was very sore. (Her)
H. _____ painted her apartment. (Mrs. Silver)
I. _____ apartment was painted. (Mrs. Silver)
J. The teacher wrote _____ name on the board. (his)
K. _____ ate his lunch. (Mr. Koo)
L. My _____ bill is paid. (brother)
M. _____ spent her money. (Angela)
N. Which is _____ coat? (your)
O. _____ shoes are old. (My)
P. Did your sister hurt _____ hand? (her)
Q. The _____ desk is near the door. (teacher)
R. _____ desk is near the door. (His)
S. _____ apartment is on the third floor. (Ms. Vega)
T. Is the _____ office open today? (doctor)
U. Is _____ office open today? (his)
V. _____ head hurts. (Mike)
W. _____ has a headache. (Mike)

## Adjectives

Adjectives describe a person, place, or thing (a noun):

    a tall building    a good dinner    a happy day
    the nice woman    some bad weather    a hot bath
    a sore hand    a long ride    some cheap food

Notice that the adjective comes before the noun.

**WRITE SENTENCES WITH THE ADJECTIVES.**

A. _____Yesterday was a warm day._____ (yesterday—warm)
B. _____ (car—old)
C. _____ (scratch—small)
D. _____ (coat—red)
E. _____ (headache—bad)
F. _____ (nose—stuffy)
G. _____ (radio—new)
H. _____ (scissors—dull)
I. _____ (knife—sharp)
J. _____ (sweater—soft)
K. _____ (back—sore)
L. _____ (arm—stiff)

## Intensifiers and Qualifiers

Words like sort of, kind of, pretty, really, and very help describe adjectives.

| Degree of Intensity | | |
|---|---|---|
| low | Their house is sort of small. | The weather is kind of bad. |
| moderate to high | Lee has a pretty bad cold. | |
| high | Pete has a really sore back. | |
| | That's a very tall building. | |

**ADD AN INTENSIFIER TO EACH SENTENCE.**
Use sort of, kind of, pretty, really, and very.

A.    That is a tall building.  (very)    That is a very tall building.

B. We had a good dinner. (really) _____
C. My back feels stiff. (kind of) _____
D. We went for a long ride. (pretty) _____
E. He feels sick. (sort of) _____
F. This sweater is soft. (really) _____
G. That chair is old. (pretty) _____
H. He has a small bruise on his knee. (very) _____
I. It's warm outside. (kind of) _____
J. Kim is shy. (sort of) _____
K. My arm is sore. (really) _____
L. She has a bad toothache. (very) _____
M. This knife is dull. (kind of) _____
N. I have a sharp pain in my neck. (pretty) _____

## Verb forms used as adjectives

The ing forms of some verbs are used as adjectives.
They describe something that continues (keeps happening):

My head is throbbing.
I have a throbbing headache.

My throat is burning.
There is a burning feeling in my throat.

Past participles of some verbs are adjectives.
Use the past participle to describe something that has happened:

Maria has broken her arm.
Her arm is broken.
She's got a broken arm.

Lan has injured his foot.
His foot is injured.
He has an injured foot.

I burned my finger.
My finger is burned.
I have a burned finger.

(Notice the different meanings of burned and burning.)

Sometimes adjectives are formed by adding a y to a verb:

> My back is stiff and my legs ache.
> I feel achy. I think I have the flu.
>
> I have red spots on my stomach. They itch.
> I have itchy red spots on my stomach.

**FILL IN THE MISSING WORDS.**
**Form an adjective by changing the verb that follows each sentence.**

- **A.** Bob can't walk on his _____ foot. (injure)
- **B.** Mike has a _____ nose. (stuff)
- **C.** The man had a _____ pain in his chest. (throb)
- **D.** That pepper's hot! I have a _____ feeling in my mouth. (burn)
- **E.** That pot is hot! I have a _____ finger. (burn).
- **F.** You should take care of that _____ ankle. (sprain)
- **G.** He finished the race with a _____ toe. (bleed)
- **H.** The x-ray showed that she had two _____ bones. (break)
- **I.** This cream will help with your _____ skin. (itch)
- **J.** I have a _____ left knee. (bruise)

# PRACTICE ON YOUR OWN

- **A.** Talk to friends. Ask them about some injuries and illnesses they have had. Ask them about their symptoms. Did they have pain? What kind of pain? Where did they feel pain—what body parts hurt?

- **B.** Practice giving advice and showing sympathy. Use this dialogue as an example:

  > YOU: What's the matter?
  > PERSON: I've got a very bad headache.
  > YOU: That's too bad! You should take some aspirin.

**C.** Listen to the radio and television ads (commercials) for medicine.
What kinds of advice do these commercials give?
What words show that they are giving advice?
Talk about some of the advice you hear.

**D.** Go to a store that sells sympathy and get well cards.
Write down some of the expressions on the cards. Ask a friend
or your teacher to explain the words you don't know.

**E.** Go to the library and look at the books on "human anatomy."
Find out some of the names of other parts of your body.

**F.** Make a chart like the one on page 20. List some illnesses
you have had. Describe the symptoms.

# UNIT 2

## WHAT DID THE DOCTOR SAY?

IN THIS UNIT YOU WILL LEARN:

how to ask questions about clinics, doctors, and specialists
how to make an appointment
how to understand a doctor's directions during a physical examination
how to talk about your habits
how to tell how often you do something (frequency)
how to talk about length of time (duration)
how to ask for and give an opinion
how to talk about fear and worry
how to fill out a medical history form

As you go through this unit, notice the following:

**in, during, on, at, before, after, from, until, about**
**never, rarely, seldom, hardly ever, sometimes, often, usually, always**
how long . . .? how often . . .?
**for** and **since**
Have/has been + verb + ing (continuous present perfect)
**used to** + verb (habitual past tense)

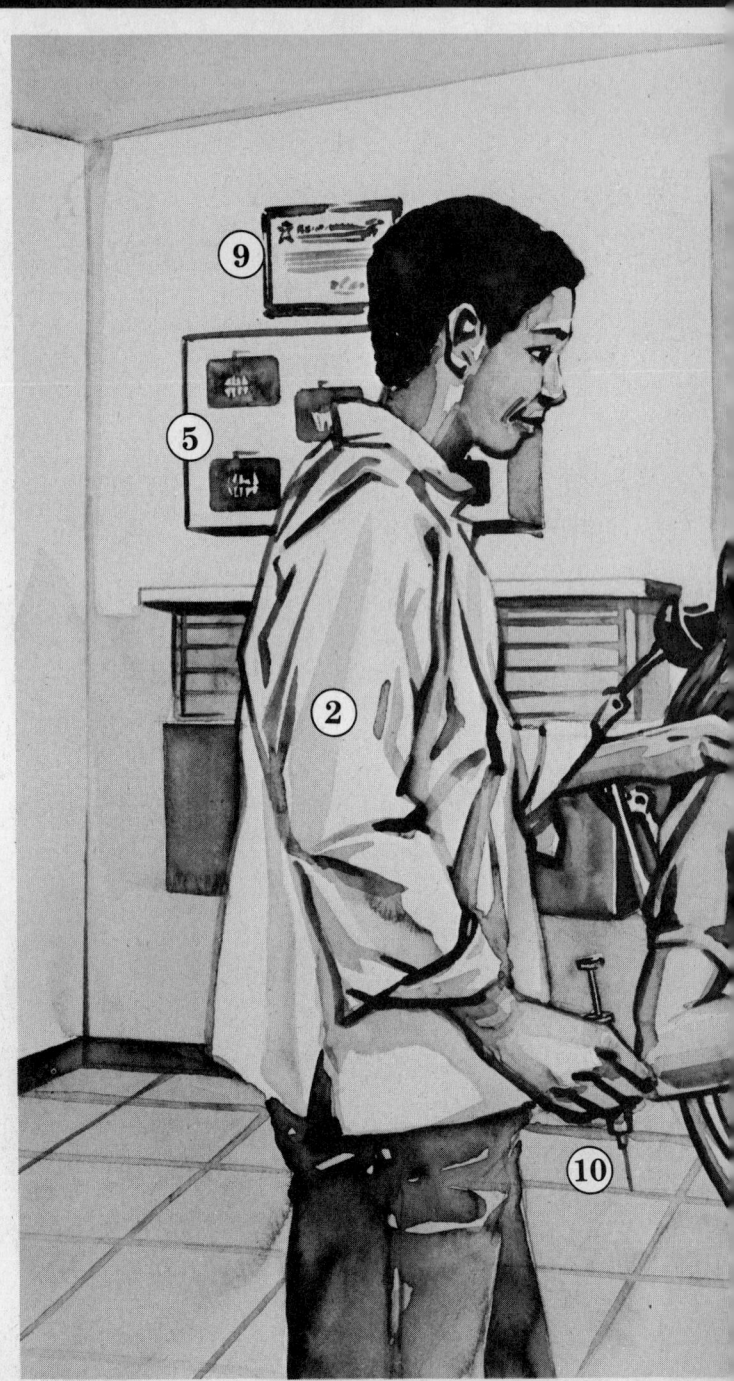

**LOOK AT THE PICTURE.**
**Find these things in the picture.**

1. dentist
2. dental hygienist
3. drill
4. x-ray machine
5. x-rays
6. tray
7. instruments
8. drinking fountain
9. diploma
10. hypodermic needle

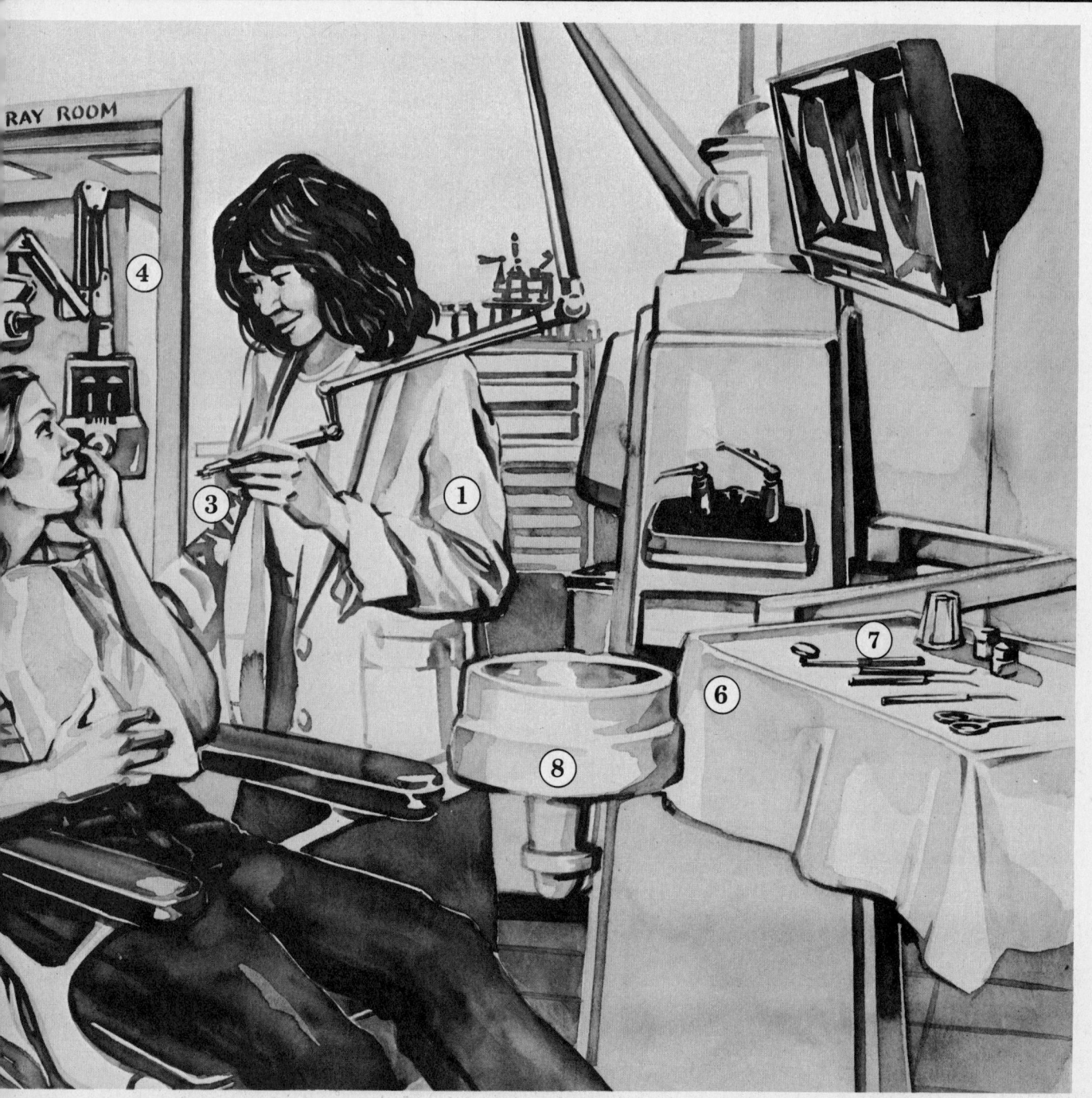

35

# TALK TOPICS

**LOOK AT THE PICTURES.
Talk about what you see.**

What is this place?
What is the dentist doing?
What is the dental hygienist doing?
How does the patient feel?

Talk about your experiences with a
    dentist or doctor.

How did you find the doctor?
Did you like the doctor?
    Why? Why not?
Did the doctor explain things to you?
Did you ask questions?
What did the doctor ask you?
Did the doctor reassure you?
Did you feel pain?
What did the doctor do to make you feel
    better?

What is a diploma?
What does it tell you?
Why does a doctor have a diploma in the
    office?

What are some differences between this
    picture and the first one?
Talk about what has changed.

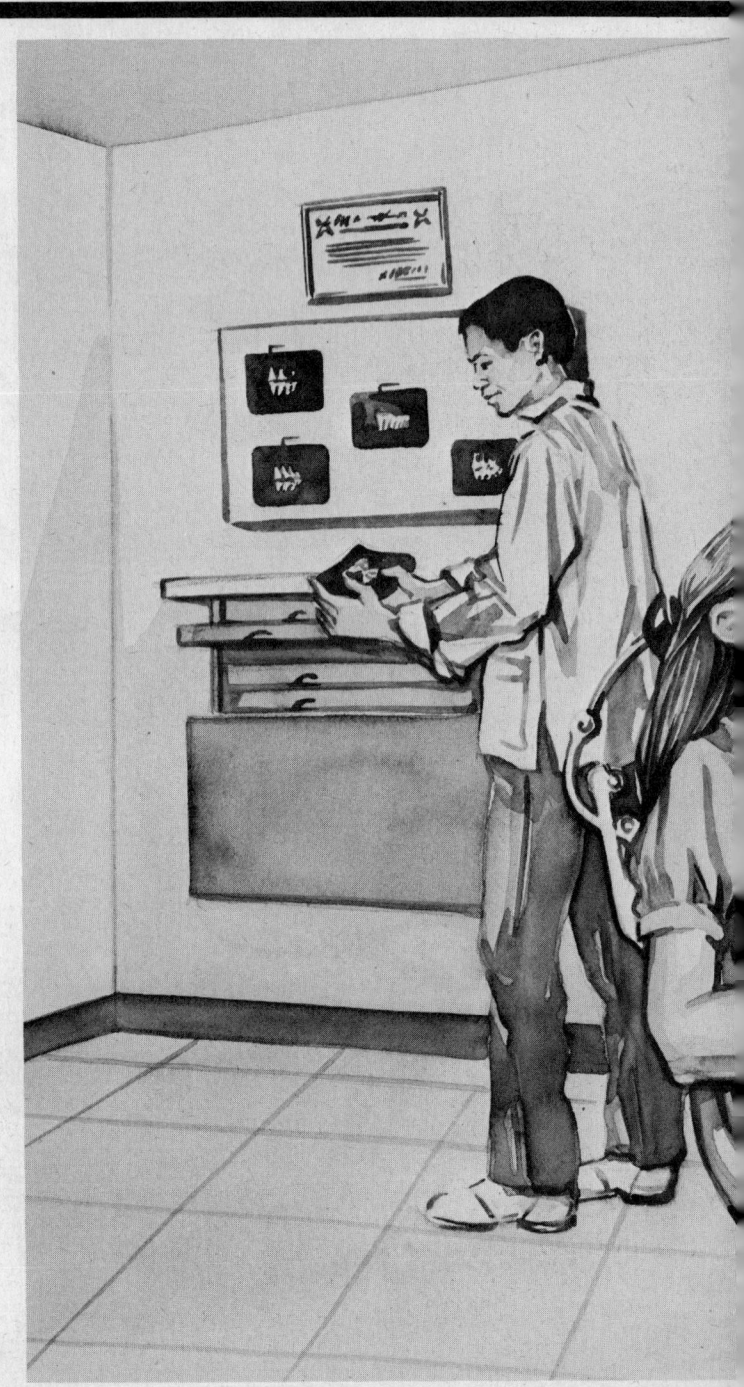

**ASK ABOUT OTHER THINGS IN THE PICTURE.**
Use these question words: <u>who</u>, <u>what</u>, <u>which</u>, <u>where</u>, <u>when</u>, <u>why</u>, and <u>how</u>.
Write your new words.

11. _____  16. _____
12. _____  17. _____
13. _____  18. _____
14. _____  19. _____
15. _____  20. _____

37

# CHOOSING A DOCTOR OR A CLINIC

What do you need to know before you go to a doctor or a clinic?

| | | |
|---|---|---|
| A. | Recommendation | Has a friend or relative been to the doctor or clinic? |
| B. | Location | Where is the doctor or clinic?  How do you get there? |
| C. | Office Hours | When can you go there? |
| D. | Fees | How much will you have to pay? |
| E. | Experience | How long has the doctor been practicing? |
| | | How long has the clinic been open? |
| F. | Hospital | What hospital is the doctor or clinic associated with? |
| G. | Specialties | Is the doctor a specialist? |
| | | What kinds of doctors are there at the clinic? |

**LISTEN TO THESE PEOPLE.**
**They are asking about a doctor or a clinic.**

**MIKE:** Can you recommend a good doctor?
**RICK:** I think Dr. Miller's great.

**CARLA:** You go to the clinic, don't you? Is it any good?
**RITA:** I like it.  They really care about the patients.

**MIKE:** How do I get to your office?
**RECEPTIONIST:** Take the D17 bus to 5th and Main Streets.

**CARLA:** Is it hard to get to the clinic?
**RITA:** No, it's easy.  Take this bus to Wilkins Avenue.

**MIKE:** Does the doctor have evening hours?

**RECEPTIONIST:** Yes, Mondays and Wednesdays from 6 to 8.

**CARLA:** Can I go to the clinic after work?

**RITA:** They stay open late on Thursdays.

**MIKE:** How much is an office visit?

**RECEPTIONIST:** $30 for the first visit and $25 for following visits.

**CARLA:** What are the fees at this clinic?

**RITA:** It depends on your income. Some people pay more than others.

**MIKE:** Doctor, why do you want to send me to a specialist?

**DOCTOR:** I'm a general practitioner. I'm referring you to a specialist who has more experience with your problem.

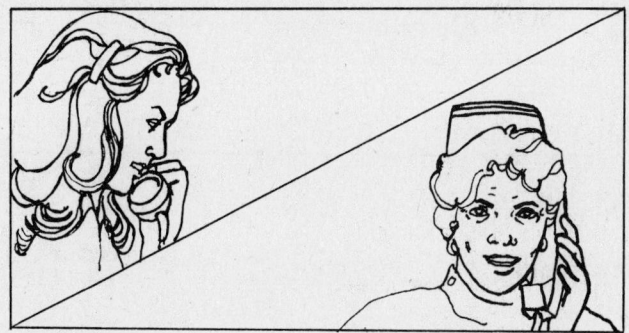

**CARLA:** Are there any specialists at the clinic?

**NURSE:** There's a pediatrician, an ophthalmologist, and a gynecologist.

**TALK TO THIS PERSON.**
**You are a patient.**
**Practice asking questions. You are talking to a doctor's receptionist.**

PATIENT: _____ (location)
RECEPTIONIST: Take bus number 5 to the corner of Market and 7th. Our office is on the second floor.

PATIENT: _____ (office hours)
RECEPTIONIST: Hours are Monday, Wednesday, and Friday from 8 to 2, and Thursdays from 6 to 8.

PATIENT: _____ (fees)
RECEPTIONIST: We charge $25 for the first visit, and $20 for following visits.

PATIENT: _____ (hospital)
RECEPTIONIST: Dr. Miller is associated with Kingsway Hospital.

**TRY IT ON YOUR OWN.**
**Practice with a friend.**
**Ask about the doctor or clinic your friend goes to.**
**The other person answers.**

YOU: _____ (location)
PERSON: _____

YOU: _____ (hours)
PERSON: _____

YOU: _____ (fees)
PERSON: _____

YOU: _____ (specialists)
PERSON: _____

YOU: _____ (hospital)
PERSON: _____

**LOOK AT THESE PICTURES.**
They show doctors who are specialists and what they do.

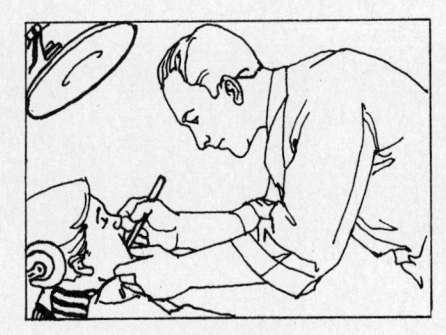

Dentist
care of teeth

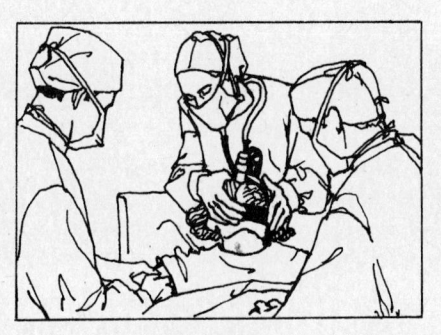

Surgeon
major operations

Gynecologist/Obstetrician
women's health problems;
delivers babies

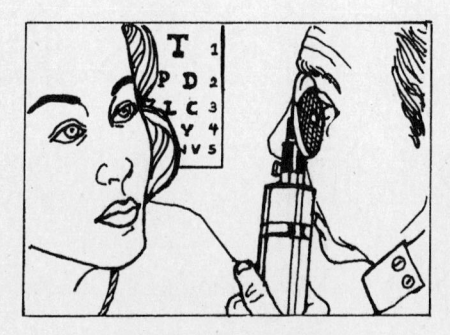

Ophthalmologist
care of eyes

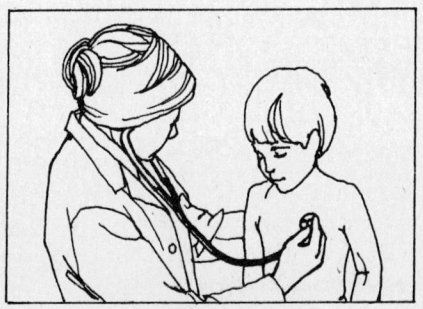

Pediatrician
children's health

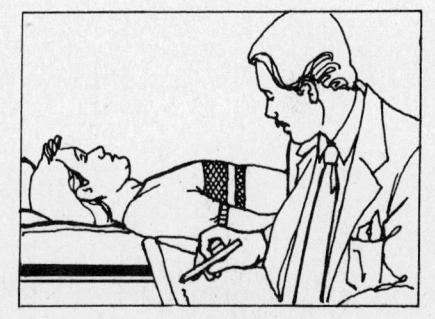

Psychiatrist
mental health

**TELL WHICH SPECIALIST YOU SHOULD SEE IF:**

A. You are going to have a baby. _____

B. You have trouble seeing the words in this book. _____

C. You have a toothache. _____

D. Your three-year-old daughter is sick. _____

E. You don't know who you are. _____

**TALK TOPICS**

Here is a list of some other kinds of specialists:

| | | | |
|---|---|---|---|
| acupuncturist | dermatalogist | neurologist | osteopath |
| chiropractor | naturopath | orthopedist | podiatrist |

A. Do you know these other specialists?
B. What do these doctors do?
C. Have you been to a specialist?

# MAKING AN APPOINTMENT

**LISTEN TO THESE PEOPLE.**
A patient is calling to make a doctor's appointment.

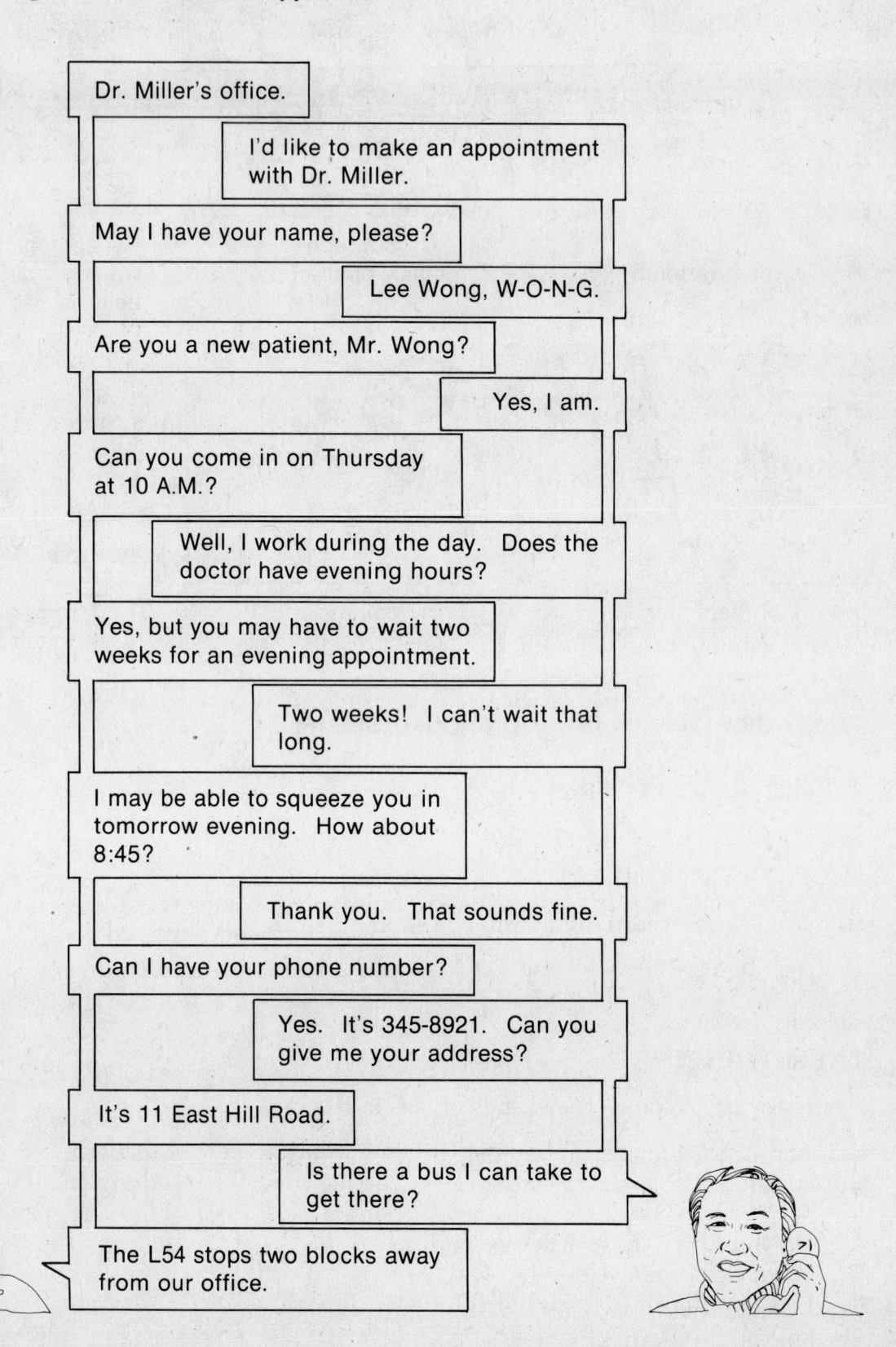

Dr. Miller's office.

I'd like to make an appointment with Dr. Miller.

May I have your name, please?

Lee Wong, W-O-N-G.

Are you a new patient, Mr. Wong?

Yes, I am.

Can you come in on Thursday at 10 A.M.?

Well, I work during the day. Does the doctor have evening hours?

Yes, but you may have to wait two weeks for an evening appointment.

Two weeks! I can't wait that long.

I may be able to squeeze you in tomorrow evening. How about 8:45?

Thank you. That sounds fine.

Can I have your phone number?

Yes. It's 345-8921. Can you give me your address?

It's 11 East Hill Road.

Is there a bus I can take to get there?

The L54 stops two blocks away from our office.

Here are some ways to talk about time:

The doctor can see you anytime in February.
When can I come in on Monday?

The doctor can see you at 12:30.
I'd like to come in about 3.
Can't I come in before 10:00?
The doctor is free today after 2:30.
We are open from 9 until 4.

I'll be very busy during that month.


**FILL IN THE MISSING WORDS.**
**Use in, on, at, about, before, after, from, until, or during.**


A.   The doctor can see you anytime _____ July.

   I'll be very busy _____ the summer.

B.   The clinic is open _____ 8:30 _____ 5:30, Mondays through Thursdays.

   Can I come in _____ Friday?

   Yes. _____ Fridays, we are open _____ 7:00.

C.   The dentist is free _____ 2 today.

   Does she have any time _____ 2?   My tooth is killing me!

   One moment, please.   Yes, she can see you _____ 9.


**TRY IT IN CLASS.**
**Practice making an appointment with a dentist.   Use this information.**

> DR. T. SMITH, DDS
> HOURS:   M-F 9:30-4
>             S    10-1
> By appointment only.

```
         PATIENT:  ask for an appointment
    RECEPTIONIST:  tell when office is open
         PATIENT:  ask to come in Thursday
    RECEPTIONIST:  make appointment for 2:00
         PATIENT:  say you'll be busy that afternoon; ask about
                   a morning appointment
    RECEPTIONIST:  make an appointment before 10:00
```

# TAKING A PHYSICAL EXAMINATION

**LOOK AT THESE PICTURES.**
They show doctors giving directions to patients during physical examinations.

Please step on the scale.
I want to check your weight and measure your height.

Please roll up your sleeve.
I'm going to take a blood sample.

Please hold out your arm.
I want to check your blood pressure.

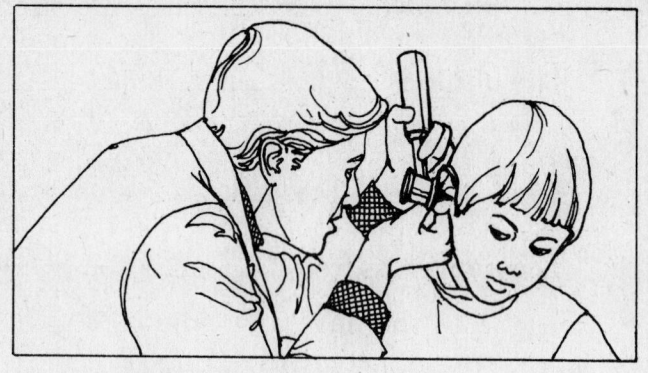

Please hold your head still.
Let me check your ears, nose, and throat.

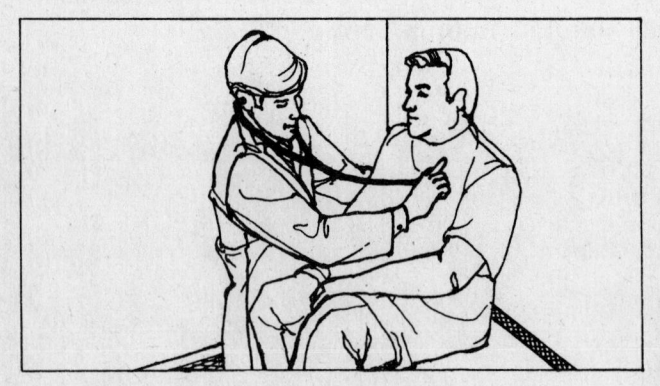

Please sit up on the table.
I'm going to use this stethoscope to listen to your heart and lungs.

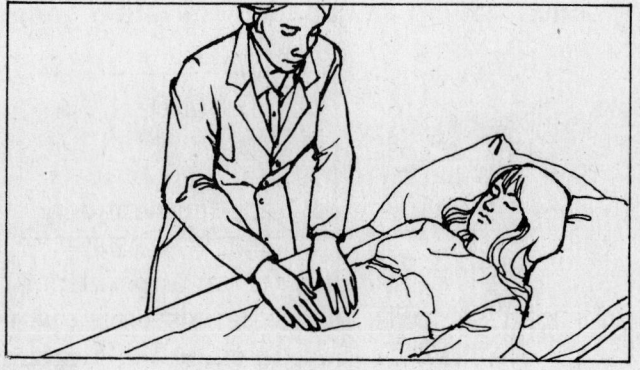

Please lie down on the table.
Tell me if you feel any pain here.

**FILL IN THE MISSING WORDS.**
**Practice using commands.**

A. Please _____ on the scale.

   I want to _____ your weight.

B. Now I'm _____ to measure your height.

C. _____ your head still. _____ me check your ears.

D. Please _____ down on the table.

   Tell me if you _____ any pain here.

E. Please _____ up on the table.

   I _____ to check your knee.

F. I'm going to _____ a blood sample now.

   Please _____ up your sleeve.

G. Please hold _____ your arm.

   I want to _____ your _____ pressure.

**TRY IT IN CLASS.**
**You are a doctor.**
**What direction would you give if you wanted to:**

A. check a patient's weight? _____

B. listen to a patient's heart? _____

C. take a blood sample? _____

D. check a patient's blood pressure? _____

E. check a patient's ears? _____

F. measure a patient's height? _____

**TALK TOPICS**

A. What is a stethoscope?
B. How does a doctor take a blood sample?
C. What is blood pressure?
D. Did you ever have a physical examination?
   What did the doctor do?
E. How much do you weigh? How tall are you?

# TALKING ABOUT HABITS

**LISTEN TO THESE PEOPLE.**
They are talking about some of their habits.

Do you ever eat chocolate?

No, I never eat it. I think I'm allergic to it.

Do you often have trouble sleeping?

I sometimes have trouble, but not very often.

I always drink at least six cups of coffee a day.

Really? I hardly ever drink coffee. I usually drink water.

I usually get home from work about 6:00. I'm rarely late.

Yeah? I'm seldom home before 7:00.

**TRY IT IN CLASS.**
Practice talking about habits.
Use these words: <u>never</u>, <u>rarely</u>, <u>seldom</u>, <u>hardly ever</u>, <u>sometimes</u>, <u>often</u>, <u>usually</u>, <u>always</u>.

A. Do you see a doctor often?
B. Do you often go for a walk?
C. Do you ever drink wine? When do you drink it?
D. Do you often have headaches?
E. Are you often late for your English class?
F. Do you go to see the dentist often?
G. Do you ever skip lunch?

**LISTEN TO THESE PEOPLE.**
They are talking about their habits.

How much coffee do you drink?
I drink about six cups a day.

How many hours a week do you work?
I work 35 hours a week.

How much do you smoke?
I used to smoke two packs a day, but now I smoke one.

**FILL IN THE MISSING WORDS.**
Practice talking about habits.

A. How _____ do you weigh?

I _____ to weigh 165 pounds, but now I _____ 170.

B. How _____ coffee do you _____ ?

I drink only two cups _____ day.

C. How _____ cups of coffee do you drink?

I used to _____ eight cups _____ day. _____ I never have coffee.

D. How _____ hours a week do you work?

I only work 20 hours _____ week.

E. How _____ times _____ week do you see the doctor?

I _____ him twice _____ week.

F. How _____ hours do you sleep a night?

I used to _____ 8 hours _____ night, but _____ I usually _____ 6 hours.

47

# TALKING ABOUT WHEN THINGS STARTED

**LISTEN TO THESE PEOPLE.**
They are talking about how long they have had a pain.

How long have you felt this way?

For a few days. I've been sick since Monday morning.

How long have you had this pain?

Since last night. It started out as a dull ache, but now it's killing me.

How long does the pain last?

Only a few minutes. It comes and goes.

When did your tooth start to hurt?

A couple of weeks ago. But it only hurts every once in a while.

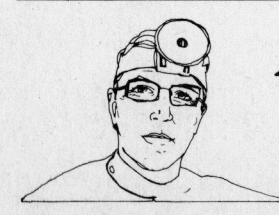

When did you first notice this pain?

It didn't bother me until Saturday afternoon.

Have you ever felt this way before?

Yes. It's happened twice before. Once when I was 12, and once about two years ago.

> How often does this happen?

> It always happens after I eat tomatoes.

**FILL IN THE MISSING WORDS.**
**Practice talking about time.**

A. How _____ does the pain last?

　　Only a few minutes. It _____ and goes.

B. How long _____ you had a fever?

　　_____ last night.

C. _____ did your knee start _____ hurt?

　　A couple _____ weeks ago. But it only hurts every

　　_____ in a while.

D. When did you first _____ this pain?

　　Three weeks _____ . It _____ as a dull ache, but

　　now it's _____ me.

E. Have you _____ felt this pain _____ ?

　　Yes. _____ two years ago.

F. How _____ does this happen?

　　It _____ happens on Monday morning.

**TRY IT IN CLASS.**
**One student is a doctor. The other is a patient.**

DOCTOR:　Ask patient to tell you his problem.
PATIENT:　Tell doctor what kind of pain you have and where the pain is.
DOCTOR:　Ask when the pain started.
PATIENT:　Tell when the pain started.
DOCTOR:　Ask how often patient has the pain.
PATIENT:　Tell how often you have the pain.

49

**LISTEN TO THESE PEOPLE.**
They are talking about length of time (duration).

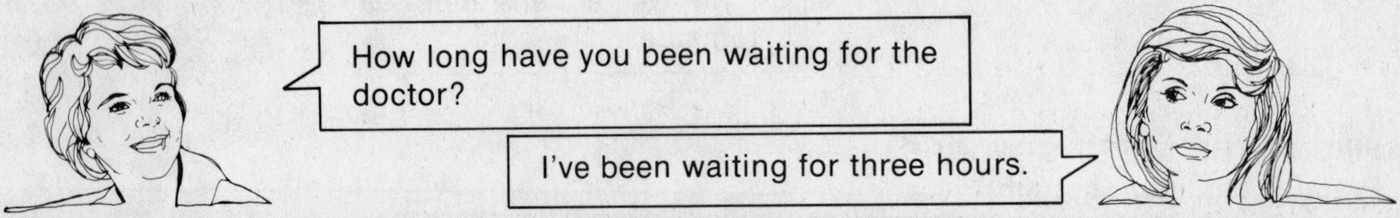

How long have you been waiting for the doctor?

I've been waiting for three hours.

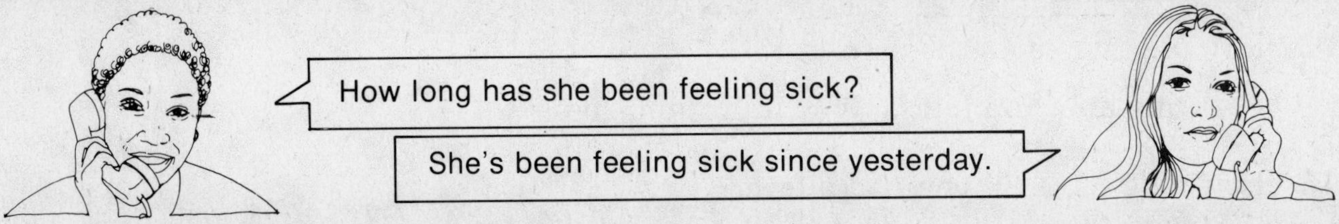

How long has she been feeling sick?

She's been feeling sick since yesterday.

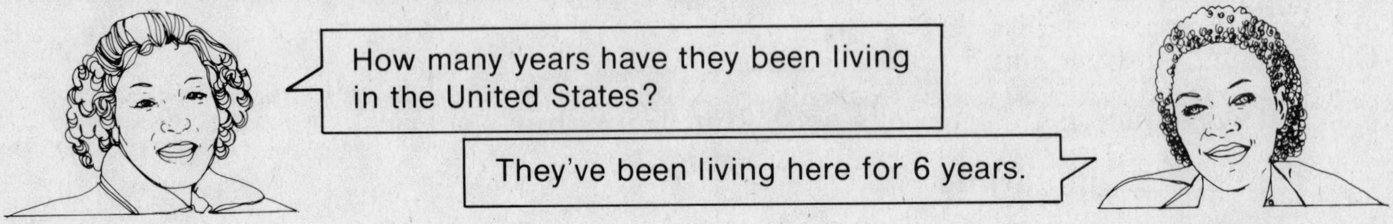

How many years have they been living in the United States?

They've been living here for 6 years.

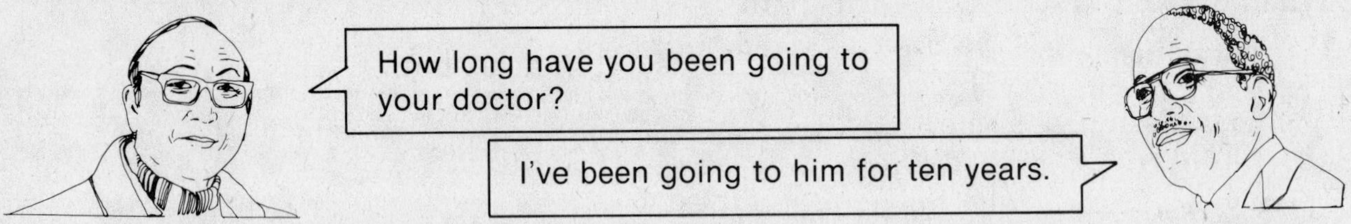

How long have you been going to your doctor?

I've been going to him for ten years.

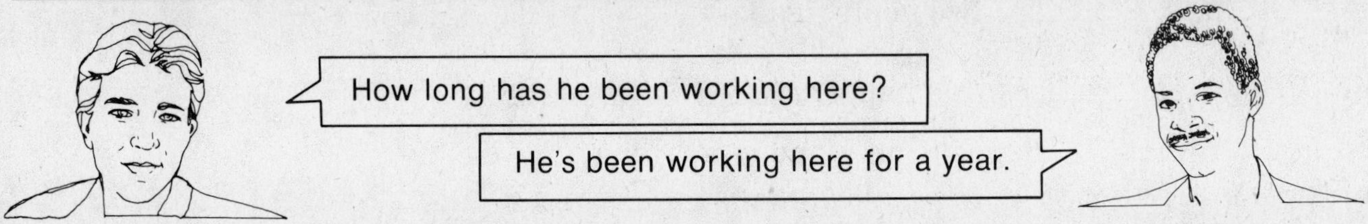

How long has he been working here?

He's been working here for a year.

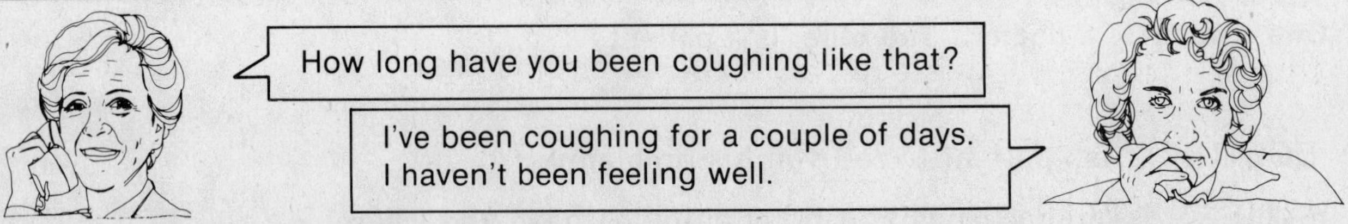

How long have you been coughing like that?

I've been coughing for a couple of days. I haven't been feeling well.

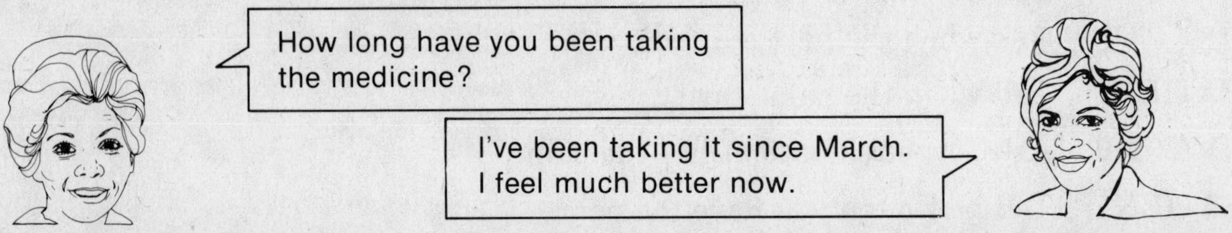

How long have you been taking the medicine?

I've been taking it since March. I feel much better now.

**FILL IN THE MISSING WORDS.**
Practice talking about length of time.

A. How long __have__ you __been feeling__ this way? (feel)
I __'ve been feeling__ this way __for__ two days.

B. How long _____ your tooth _____ you? (hurt)
It _____ me _____ Monday morning.

C. How long _____ you _____ to this clinic? (come)
I _____ here _____ a year now.

D. How long _____ he _____ ? (smoke)
He _____ now _____ thirty years.

E. How many years _____ they _____ here? (work)
They _____ here _____ almost five years.

F. How long _____ she _____ for the dentist? (wait)
She _____ for him _____ noon.

G. How long _____ it _____ ? (rain)
It _____ heavily _____ last night.

**TALK TO THESE PEOPLE.**
Answer the questions using __have/has been__ + a verb + __ing__.

PERSON: How long have you been studying English?
YOU: _____

PERSON: How long have you been living in the United States?
YOU: _____

PERSON: How long have you been sitting here?
YOU: _____

PERSON: How long have you been reading this book?
YOU: _____

# ASKING YOUR DOCTOR FOR AN OPINION

**LISTEN TO THESE PEOPLE.**
The patients are asking the doctors for their opinions.

Your blood pressure is a little high.

Is it serious? Should I do anything for it?

No, it's nothing to worry about.

---

You should stop smoking.

I know. Do you think that is what is causing my problem?

Yes, I do. If you keep smoking, you'll make it worse.

---

I want to run some more tests.

Why? Is anything wrong?

You may have an ulcer. The tests will tell us for sure.

---

Do you think I should have an operation?

No. I don't recommend surgery in your case.

But what will happen if I don't have an operation? Will I ever get better?

These problems usually go away after a few months. I'll tell you if I think you need surgery.

**FILL IN THE MISSING WORDS.**
**Practice asking and giving an opinion.**

A. I _____ you to see a specialist.

   Why? _____ anything wrong?

   The specialist _____ tell me if _____ wrong.

B. Your tonsils _____ a little swollen.

   Do you _____ I _____ have a tonsillectomy?

   No. The swelling usually goes down.

C. Your daughter _____ the mumps.

   _____ it contagious? _____ I keep her at home for a few days?

   Yes, but it's nothing to _____ about.

D. You _____ lose weight.

   I know. _____ you think that is what is _____ my problem?

   Yes. _____ you don't lose weight, you'll make it _____ .

E. Doctor, what will _____ if I don't have an operation?

   _____ I ever _____ better?

   Don't worry. I'll _____ you if I think you _____ surgery.

F. Doctor, _____ I _____ an operation?

   No, I don't _____ surgery.


**TRY IT IN CLASS.**
**Practice asking a doctor for an opinion.**
**Ask about:**

A. your high blood pressure
B. needing an operation
C. needing glasses
D. treating your son's chickenpox
E. treating your sore back
F. getting better

# TALKING ABOUT CERTAINTY

**LISTEN TO THESE PEOPLE.**
**They are talking about how certain or uncertain they are.**

I think your headaches may be caused by eyestrain.

Do you think I need glasses?

I can't be sure. You should see an opthalmologist, an eye doctor.

---

You're farsighted. You need glasses.

Are you sure, doctor?

Yes, I'm sure. The eye examination shows you need them.

Do you think my eyes will get worse?

I don't think so, but I can't be sure.

---

I wonder if I'm allergic to the medicine you gave me.

I'm not sure, but you could be allergic to it. Let's play it safe and change to another kind.

---

You should probably stop drinking any kind of alcohol until you're over this illness.

Do I have to stop drinking completely? Could I have a glass of wine with dinner?

Perhaps one glass of wine with dinner wouldn't hurt. But I think you'd be better off if you didn't drink at all.

54

> I think you may be allergic to cats.
>
> How will you know for sure?
>
> I'll have to do some tests.

**TRY IT IN CLASS.**
**Practice talking about certainty.**

A. Is it going to rain?
   (perhaps) _____

B. Do I need glasses?
   (not sure) _____

C. I think you may be allergic to berries.
   (know/sure?) _____

D. I think your bad stomachaches may be caused by an ulcer.
   (think/need/operation?) _____

E. Should I lose some weight?
   (should/probably) _____

F. What's wrong, doctor?
   (ankle/may/broken) _____

G. You ought to stop eating chocolate.
   (have to/completely?) _____

H. You're anemic. You need more iron.
   (think so?) _____

I. I wonder if I need glasses. My eyes are hurting me.
   (can't/sure; should/see/ophthalmologist) _____

J. You should probably stop drinking coffee until your stomach feels better.
   (could/one cup/a day?) _____

55

# TALKING ABOUT FEAR AND WORRY

**LISTEN TO THESE PEOPLE.**
One person is showing fear or worry.
The other person is reassuring.

—I'm worried about going to the dentist.
—Why?
—I'm afraid he'll hurt me.
—Don't worry. He'll give you a shot to ease the pain.

—I'm afraid of pain. Will it hurt much?
—No, you'll hardly feel it.
—Are you sure?
—Yes. Just try to relax.

—My tooth is killing me. Will I lose it?
—No. It can be fixed.
—Will it hurt a lot?
—I'll give you a painkiller. You'll feel much better soon.

—I'm scared to go to the doctor.
—Why?
—He may tell me that I need an operation.
—I'm sure you'll be all right. I'll go with you if you want me to.

> I don't want to go to the dentist.
>
> You aren't afraid, are you?
>
> Yes, I'm scared of the drill.
>
> Don't worry. Maybe you won't have any cavities.

**FILL IN THE MISSING WORDS.**
**Practice talking about being afraid or worried.**
**Practice trying to make someone feel less afraid or worried.**

A. I'm worried _____ getting sick.

   I'm _____ you'll be _____ right.

B. I'm scared _____ go to the dentist.

   What are you afraid _____?

   I'm _____ he'll hurt _____.

   _____ worry. I'm sure it _____ hurt much.

C. I'm really scared _____ the drill.

   It'll only _____ a couple of minutes.

   Will it _____ much?

   No, you'll _____ feel it.

**TALK TO THESE PEOPLE.**
Tell them: "I'm afraid of," "I'm worried about," or "I'm scared of."

YOU: _____ I'm afraid of the dentist. _____ (the dentist)

PERSON: Don't worry. I'm sure he won't hurt you too much.

YOU: _____ (being sick)

PERSON: I'm sure you'll be all right.

YOU: _____ (feeling pain)

PERSON: It'll be over soon. You'll hardly feel it.

YOU: _____ (losing a tooth)

PERSON: Don't worry. It can be fixed.

57

**FILL IN THIS MEDICAL HISTORY FORM.**
Write information about yourself.
Talk about the words you don't know in class.

## MEDICAL HISTORY

Please print

Name _____   Date of Birth _____
    (last)    (first)                               mo/day/yr

Address _____   Telephone _____

Please check (√) any of these problems that you have had:

Please check (√) any of these diseases that you have had:

Frequent colds _____
Frequent sore throats _____
Frequent headaches _____
Allergies _____
Stomach problems _____
Kidney problems _____
High blood pressure _____
Anemia _____
Mental depression _____
Serious injuries _____

Chickenpox _____
Measles _____
Rubella _____
Mumps _____
Scarlet Fever _____
Polio _____
Whooping Cough _____
Tuberculosis _____
Diabetes _____
Hepatitis _____

Are you taking any medications? _____

Which ones? _____
_____

Are you allergic to any medications? _____

Which ones? _____
_____

Have you had any operations? _____
Please describe them briefly and give the dates:
_____
_____
_____

Have you ever been hospitalized for any other reason? _____
Please describe briefly and give the dates:
_____
_____

# CLOSE-UP ON LANGUAGE

## For and since with time expressions

Use for to talk about how long: (for + length of time):

for three minutes        I've been waiting for three minutes
for five hours           He's been reading for five hours.
for eight years          We've been living here for eight years.

Use since to talk about the time something started (since + point in time):

since twelve o'clock     It's been raining since twelve o'clock.
since this morning       He's been watching TV since this morning.
since 1980               They've been coming here since 1980.

**FILL IN THE MISSING WORDS.**
**Use for or since.**

A. I've been going to that restaurant _____ two years.

B. Haven't you seen her _____ your birthday?

C. They've been talking _____ an hour.

D. Are you staying at the beach _____ a month?

E. The band has been playing _____ eight o'clock.

F. My leg has been hurting _____ a week.

G. I've been going to this doctor _____ I was ten.

H. She's been working there _____ July.

I. We've been looking for a new apartment _____ four months.

J. I've been studying English _____ 1981.

K. I've had a headache _____ for the last two hours.

L. I haven't seen you _____ a long time.

M. Maria hasn't been here _____ this morning.

N. Ted's operation lasted _____ four hours.

O. He has been studying _____ eight o'clock this morning.

P. Tran hasn't seen a doctor _____ 1976.

Q. I went to that school _____ three years.

R. My back has been killing me _____ last Thursday.

S. Alfredo has been living in that house _____ July.

## Using have/has been + a verb + ing
### (continuous present perfect)

I have (I've) been waiting for two hours.
He has (he's) been waiting since noon.
You have (you've) been waiting for a long time.

**FORM SENTENCES.**
Use the continuous present perfect tense (have/has been + verb + ing).

A. I/work/here/three years
   I've been working here for three years.

B. She/study/eight o'clock
   She's been studying since eight o'clock.

C. We/wait/ten thirty

D. They/work/nine o'clock

E. He/smoke/ten years

F. You/live/there/two months

G. I/feel/sick/two days

H. She/go/to school/last year

I. He/play/piano/1970

J. We/look/for you/fifteen minutes

K. Mike/back/bother/Saturday

## Question form of the continuous present perfect tense

Have you been waiting long?  How long have you been waiting?
Has it been raining all day?  How many hours has it been raining?
Has she been feeling sick?  Who has been feeling sick?
Have they been looking for me?  How long have they been looking for me?

**LOOK AT THE ANSWERS. ASK THE QUESTIONS.**
**Use the continuous present perfect tense.**

A. _____How long have you been teaching English?_____

I've been teaching English for five years.

B. _____

She's been waiting for fifteen minutes.

C. _____

Rita has been working there for a year.

D. _____

We have been living in this building since 1970.

E. _____

My tooth has been aching since last night.

F. _____

He's been drinking coffee for fifteen years.

G. _____

I've been taking this medicine since May.

H. _____

The sun has been shining all day.

I. _____

They've been talking for about three hours.

J. _____

You've been sleeping since yesterday.

K. _____

Mike has been studying English for two years.

## The negative form of the continuous present perfect tense

I have not been going to the movies lately.  (I haven't been going)
He has not been paying the rent on time.  (He hasn't been paying)
You have not been working hard this month.  (You haven't been working)
They have not been seeing each other much.  (They haven't been seeing)

**ANSWER THESE QUESTIONS.**
**Start each answer with No.**

A. Have you been thinking about home a lot?
   No, I haven't been thinking about home too much.

B. Have they been visiting you often?

C. Has she been feeling sick this week?

D. Has it been snowing since last night?

E. Have we been talking for three hours?

F. Has he been calling you every day?

G. Have you been worrying about the hospital a lot?

H. Has the phone been ringing all morning?

I. Has the teacher been looking for me?

J. Have I been spending too much money for food?

K. Have you been getting enough sleep at night?

## Used to + verb (habitual past)

Used to shows that something was done in the past, but not now:

    I used to smoke, but I don't anymore.
    He used to live in China, but now he lives in the U.S.
    We used to eat at that restaurant before it closed.
    They used to swim every day when they lived near the lake.

Don't confuse this with be + used to (be familiar with, accustomed to, not surprised by):

    I am used to sleeping late.
    They're used to Mexican food.

**FORM ONE SENTENCE FROM TWO.**
**Change the verb from simple past to habitual past with used to.**

**A.** She took the bus. (when) She worked downtown.
        She used to take the bus when she worked downtown.

**B.** They lived upstairs. (before) They moved.
        They used to live upstairs before they moved.

**C.** I drank a lot of coffee. (but) Now I drink tea.

**D.** I drove to work. (before) The price of gas went up.

**E.** We went to the clinic. (but) Now we go to Dr. Olsen.

**F.** He ate a lot of bread. (before) The doctor told him to lose weight.

**G.** You were fat. (before) You went on a diet.

**H.** She went to school. (but) Now she goes to work.

**FILL IN THE MISSING WORDS.**
Choose a form of the verb. Tell why you chose it.

A. I <u>am calling</u> about the ad in today's paper. (call)
B. He _____ Marta on the corner. (see)
C. We usually _____ to the clinic. (go)
D. Tom _____ a bad cold last week. (have)
E. I _____ sick all week. (feel)
F. I _____ an hour to see Dr. Brown. (wait)
G. They _____ to eat dinner in that restaurant. (like)
H. I _____ the medicine since March. (take)
I. He _____ in the factory for 12 years. (work)
J. She _____ shopping this Saturday. (go)
K. That doctor _____ too much. (charge)
L. They _____ in the U.S. for six months now. (live)
M. I _____ to go to the movies, but I was busy. (want)
N. You _____ very good in that suit. (look)
O. John _____ tomorrow. (swim)
P. Maria _____ to Puerto Rico last week. (go)

**FILL IN THE MISSING WORD.**
Practice using <u>in</u>, <u>during</u>, <u>on</u>, <u>at</u>, <u>before</u>, <u>after</u>, <u>from</u>, <u>until</u>, <u>about</u>.

A. I'll meet you _____ one o'clock.
B. The store is open _____ 10 _____ 6.
C. Your appointment is _____ Monday _____ 2:30.
D. His birthday is _____ February.
E. When can I come in _____ Wednesday?
F. He's very busy _____ the summer.
G. I think the movie starts _____ 7:30.
H. Is his office closed _____ Saturdays?
I. No, his office is open _____ 1:00.

# PRACTICE ON YOUR OWN

A. Talk to your friends about their doctors.
   Ask them these questions about their doctors:

   1. What do you like about the doctor?
   2. What don't you like about the doctor?
   3. Is the doctor easy to see?
   4. Do you have to wait a long time for him or her?
   5. Does the doctor charge a lot?
   6. How does the doctor treat you?

B. Ask your friends about health clinics.
   Is there a mental health clinic in your neighborhood?
   Is there a drug and alcohol clinic?
   Is there a birth control clinic?
   What are these clinics like?

C. What are you worried about?  Make a list of your worries.
   What are you afraid of?  Make a list of your fears.
   Talk to someone about your worries and fears.  Ask them what
   they are worried about or afraid of.  Give them reassurance
   (say something to help them feel less worried or afraid).

D. Have you been in a hospital in the U.S.?  Talk to someone
   who has been in a hospital.  Ask them to tell you about it.
   Ask these questions:

   1. Why were you in the hospital?
   2. How long were you in the hospital?
   3. Did the doctors treat you well?
   4. Did the nurses and other hospital workers treat
      you well?
   5. How much did it cost?

E. Ask someone to recommend a dentist and an ophthalmologist.
   Make an appointment to have your teeth and your eyes examined.
   How much does an examination cost?

# UNIT 3

## WHICH MEDICINE SHOULD I TAKE?

IN THIS UNIT YOU WILL LEARN:

how to talk to a doctor about prescriptions
how to understand the labels on medicines
how to get a prescription filled
how to ask a druggist for advice about over-the-counter medicines
how to compare name brand and store brand medicines
how to understand warnings and cautions
how to find out about treatments that work without medicines

As you go through this unit, notice the following:

**as . . . as** phrases for comparing
other uses for question words
**to** and **for** to talk about a reason or purpose
**this, that, these, those**
**at, in, for, on, to, with, about, between**
**while, since, before, after, if**

**LOOK AT THE PICTURE.**
Find these things in the picture.

1. drugstore
2. pharmacist/druggist
3. prescription counter
4. medicines
5. aspirin
6. nasal sprays
7. cough syrups
8. antacids
9. vitamins
10. bandages

# TALK TOPICS

**LOOK AT THE PICTURES.**
**Talk about what you see.**

What is this place?
What can you buy here?
What is the pharmacist doing?
What are the customers doing?
What is a prescription?

Have you used any of the products that
    are shown in this picture?
Which things have you used?
Which things haven't you used?
How did you find out about how to use
    these products?

What do you do when you have a
    headache?  a sore throat?  a
    stomachache?  a cough?

What are some differences between this
    picture and the first one?
Talk about what has changed.

**ASK ABOUT OTHER THINGS IN THE PICTURE.**
Use these question words: <u>who</u>, <u>what</u>, <u>where</u>, <u>when</u>, <u>which</u>, <u>how</u>.
Write your new words.

11. _____   16. _____
12. _____   17. _____
13. _____   18. _____
14. _____   19. _____
15. _____   20. _____

69

# UNDERSTANDING PRESCRIPTION MEDICINE

**LISTEN TO THESE PEOPLE.**
**The doctor is prescribing medicine for a patient.**

You need an antibiotic to help fight the infection in your chest.

Remember I'm allergic to penicillin.

I remember. This is for tetracycline. Take this prescription to a drugstore. Ask the pharmacist to fill it for you.

How much medicine do I take?

One capsule three times a day. Take them with your meals.

---

Here's a prescription for your allergy. This antihistamine will help your sneezing and teary eyes.

How often should I take it?

Take one tablet every four hours. The directions will be on the label.

I'm still taking the other medicine you gave me. Is it safe to keep taking it with this new medicine?

Yes, it's safe.

Thank you, Doctor. I'll go to the drugstore as soon as possible.

**TALK TOPICS**

A. Has your doctor prescribed medicine for you? What did you take it for? How often did you take it?

B. Are you allergic to any kind of medicine?

C. Why must you get a prescription for some kinds of medicine? Do you need a prescription for all medicines?

**LOOK AT THESE LABELS.**
**They tell the patient when to take the medicine.**
**They also tell the patient how much to take.**

A.
```
WELLING DRUGS
130 Locust Ave.
Phone 777-1235
No. 2347      Dr. Katz

Yung Wong: Take
two teaspoonfuls
four times a day.
(Donnatal) 6/2/83
```

1. How much medicine should Yung take?
   _____

2. How many times a day should Yung take the medicine?
   _____

B.
```
MEDI MART
21 Bloomfield Blvd.
Phone 425-5940
No. 8567      Dr. Allen

Carmen Perez: One tablet
three times a day with
meals.  (Tetracycline)
7/5/83
```

1. When should Carmen take this medicine?
   _____

2. What is the name of the medicine?
   _____

3. How many tablets should Carmen take in one day?
   _____

C.
```
AUSTIN DRUGS
23 Middle Rd.
Phone 482-2980
No. H 376     Dr. Young

Sara Silver: One capsule
in the morning and one
at bedtime. (Steracine)
CAUTION: May cause
drowsiness. Do not drive
while taking this medicine.
8/23/84
```

1. How many times should Sara take this medicine in one day?
   _____

2. Is there anything Sara can't do while taking this medicine?
   _____

3. What does the word CAUTION mean?
   _____

D.
```
BAY PHARMACY
6914 Vale St.
Phone 631-0079
No. LZ 14     Dr. K. Samuels

Maria Vega: One tablet
every 4 hours until used
up. (Penicillin)
6/30/85       40 Tablets
```

1. Who is this medicine for?
   _____

2. How long should the person take this medicine?
   _____

# GETTING A PRESCRIPTION FILLED

**LISTEN TO THESE PEOPLE.**
**They are talking about getting prescriptions filled.**

I'd like to have this prescription filled.

Certainly. It'll be ready in a little while. Come back in a half hour.

OK. I'll do some shopping in the meantime.

---

Can you fill this prescription, please?

Sure. Would you like to wait for it or come back later?

How long will it take?

About fifteen minutes.

Then I'll wait. I'll look around the store while you fill it.

---

Here's your prescription, Mrs. Silver.

Thank you. Oh, excuse me. Can you explain what this label means?

Certainly. This part, "Caution: May cause drowsiness," means that you can get sleepy from this medicine.

Oh, I see. That's why it says "Do not drive while taking." I might fall asleep at the wheel.

That's right. The label is telling you to be careful.

**FILL IN THE MISSING WORDS.**
**Practice getting a prescription filled.**

A. I'd like to _____ this prescription _____ .

It'll be _____ in a little _____ . Can you come back _____ fifteen minutes?

Sure. In the _____ , I'll _____ some shopping.

B. Can you _____ this prescription, please?

Yes, but _____ have to wait for a _____ .

How long will it _____ ?

About a half _____ .

All right. I'll come back _____ .

C. Your _____ is ready, Mr. Wong.

What does this _____ : "Caution: May cause drowsiness. Do not drive while taking"?

It means that you can get _____ from this medicine.

Oh, I _____ . The label's _____ me to be _____ .

D. Please fill _____ prescription for me.

All right. You can come _____ for it later this afternoon.

How _____ will it take to fill?

About an hour.

Can I _____ for it? I have a sick child at home.

OK. _____ have it for you _____ soon _____ possible.

**TRY IT IN CLASS.**
**One student is a customer.**
**The other is a druggist.**

CUSTOMER: ask the druggist to fill your prescription.
DRUGGIST: tell the customer when the prescription will be ready.
CUSTOMER: tell whether you'll wait or come back.

# ASKING A DRUGGIST FOR ADVICE

**LISTEN TO THESE PEOPLE.**
They are asking for advice.

Excuse me. Can you recommend something for a stuffy nose?

The Arin Nasal Spray is pretty good.

Where can I find it?

In the middle aisle, on the right hand side.

---

What do you recommend for an upset stomach?

Well, there are a number of antacids you could use.

Which one's the best?

I can't really say which is the best. But Malinta has worked well for me.

Malinta? I'll try it. Where do you keep it?

On the bottom shelf, in front of the cash register.

---

I've got all of these mosquito bites and they really itch. Do you have anything for itchy skin?

Certainly. That Lancan Ointment on the top shelf will ease the itching.

Can I use it on my face?

Yes, but be careful not to get it in your eyes.

> There are so many vitamins. Which ones should I take?
>
> Take these daily multiple vitamins. They've got everything you need.
>
> What about these super vitamins?
>
> I don't think you need those. They're just a waste of money.

**FILL IN THE MISSING WORDS.**
**Practice asking a pharmacist for advice.**

A. _____ me. What do you _____ for a cough?

   I think Vex cough syrup is _____ good.

   Vex? Where do you _____ it?

   At the end of this aisle, on the left _____ side.

B. Can you recommend _____ for an upset stomach?

   There are a _____ of antacids you _____ use.

   Which one's the _____ ?

   I can't really say _____ is the best. RELAX has _____ well for me.

   OK. I'll _____ it. Thanks.

C. My daughter has a very _____ throat. Do you

   have _____ I can give her?

   Some throat lozenges will ease the _____ .

   Do you _____ any for children?

   Yes. The Red Tens on that _____ are very good.

**TRY IT IN CLASS.**
**One person asks for advice on what to buy for each of the problems listed below. Another person tells what he or she recommends.**

|   |   |
|---|---|
| headache | stuffy nose |
| aching muscles | upset stomach |
| cuts | fever |
| sore throat | cough |

# MAKING COMPARISONS

**LISTEN TO THESE PEOPLE.**
**They are comparing products in a drugstore.**

How come that bottle of aspirin is so much more expensive than this bottle?

One is the store brand and the other is a name brand aspirin.

Is there any difference? Is the name brand better than the store brand?

No. The store brand is as effective as the name brand. Buy the cheapest.

---

What's the difference between these two kinds of cold capsules?

Nothing. They have the same ingredients.

Why is this one cheaper than the other?

The store brand's usually not as expensive as the name brand. This name brand is the most expensive brand here.

Is the store brand always the best?

Not always. Sometimes the store brand is not as good as the name brand.

---

Which vitamins should we buy?

Get the multiple vitamins. Those super vitamins really aren't better than the multiple vitamins. Anyway, the multiple vitamins are cheaper.

Look at these comparisons:

| | |
|---|---|
| One thing compared to another | These vitamins are good. They are better than those. But they are more expensive. |
| One thing compared to more than one other thing | These vitamins are the best ones in the store. They are the most expensive brand. |

**FILL IN THE MISSING WORDS.**
**Practice making comparisons.**

A. The store brand is good. It is  better than  the name brand.  (good)

B. This bottle of cough syrup is _____ that bottle.  (big)

C. This store has the _____ prices in town.  (cheap)

D. Malinta Antacid is _____ Peptol Antacid.  (effective)

E. The store brand cold capsules are _____ the name brand.  (strong)

F. This aspirin is the _____ brand in the store.  (good)

G. The pharmacist was _____ the doctor.  (helpful)

H. This painkiller is the _____ one you can buy.  (powerful)

Look at these comparisons:

| | |
|---|---|
| Equal | The store brand is as good as the name brand. |
| Not equal | The store brand isn't as good as the name brand. |

**FILL IN THE MISSING WORDS.**
**Practice making comparisons.**
Use as _____ as.

A. The prices at Medi Mart aren't  as cheap as  at Bay Pharmacy.  (cheap)

B. The store brand is _____ the name brand.  (good)

C. Regular aspirin isn't _____ the extra strength kind.  (strong)

D. This line isn't _____ that line.  (long)

E. I think that Arin is _____ Nesfrin Nasal Spray.  (effective)

F. Your temperature isn't _____ it was yesterday.  (high)

G. The cut on my finger isn't _____ the bruise on my knee.  (painful)

H. These vitamins aren't _____ those vitamins.  (big)

77

**LISTEN TO THESE PEOPLE.**
**They are comparing products using the words <u>many</u> and <u>much</u>.**

Which bottle of vitamins should I buy?

Do they both have the same number of tablets?

Yes. The store brand has as many tablets as the name brand.

Do they have the same ingredients?

No. The store brand doesn't have as much iron as the name brand.

Well, buy the store brand anyway.

---

The store brand doesn't have as much cough syrup in it as the name brand.

You're wrong. The store brand has just as many ounces of syrup.

How much cough syrup should I take?

The dosage is different. You don't take the store brand as often.

What do you mean?

The directions on the store brand say to take it three times a day, and the name brand says four times a day.

---

Are the directions on your bottle of nose drops the same as the directions on mine?

I don't think so. The dosage is different.

What do you mean?

I don't use as many drops of mine.

78

**LOOK AT THESE PICTURES.**
**Compare the products.**
**Answer the questions.  Use as _____ as phrases.**

A.

[Store brand aspirin 100 tablets — $1.10]
[Name brand aspirin 100 tablets — $1.59]

1. Do the store brand and the name brand have the same number of tablets?  (many)
   Yes.  The store brand has as many tablets as the name brand.

2. Are they the same price? (expensive)
   No.  The store brand is not as expensive as the name brand.

B.

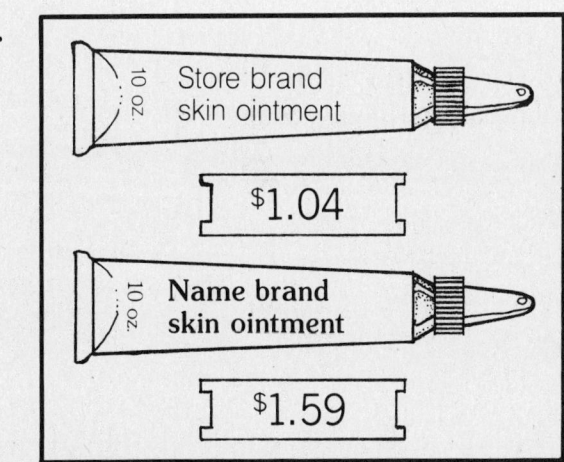

[Store brand skin ointment 10 oz. — $1.04]
[Name brand skin ointment 10 oz. — $1.59]

1. Are the store brand and the name brand the same size?  (big)
   Yes.

2. Are they the same price? (cheap)
   No.

C.

[Store brand Nose drops — 2 drops twice daily. Do not use for more than 3 days. 2 oz. — $1.49]
[Name brand Nose drops — 3 drops 3 times a day. Do not use for more than 4 days. 2 oz. — $1.49]

1. Should you use the same amount of the store brand as of the name brand?  (many)
   No.

2. Does the store brand cost the same as the name brand?  (much)
   Yes.

79

**READ THESE WARNING LABELS.**
Talk about what they mean.
Answer the questions.

A. CAUTION: Keep this and all medicine out of the reach of children. In case of accidental ingestion, contact a poison control center immediately.

1. What does "out of the reach" mean?
   _____

2. What does "accidental ingestion" mean?
   _____

B. CAUTION: For external use only. Not to be taken internally.

1. What does "external" mean?
   _____

2. Is it all right to swallow this medicine?
   _____

C. WARNINGS: Do not exceed recommended dosage. Do not use this product for more than three days. If symptoms persist, consult a physician. Do not administer to children under 2 years of age unless directed by a physician.

1. Where can you find the "recommended dosage"?
   _____

2. What does "if symptoms persist" mean?
   _____

3. What is another word for physician?
   _____

D. WARNINGS: Do not exceed recommended dosage. Persistent cough may indicate the presence of a serious condition. Consult a physician.

1. What is a "persistent cough"?
   _____

2. What may a "serious condition" be?
   _____

E. CAUTION: Do not use in or near eyes. Not for prolonged use. If conditions persist or worsen, discontinue use and consult your physician.

1. What does "prolonged use" mean?
   _____

2. What should you do if the medicine doesn't help you get better?
   _____

80

**LOOK AT THE WARNING LABELS ON PAGE 80.**
**Find the words for each of these warnings.**

A. If you don't get better, call your doctor.
   _____ If symptoms persist, consult your physician. _____

B. Don't swallow this medicine.
   _____

C. Don't use this medicine for a long time.
   _____

D. Don't take more of this medicine than the directions tell you to.
   _____

E. A cough that doesn't go away may mean that you are very sick.
   _____

F. If your symptoms get worse, stop using this medicine.
   _____

G. If someone has swallowed this medicine by mistake, call a poison control center as soon as possible.
   _____

H. Put this medicine in a place where a child can't find it.
   _____

I. Give this medicine to a small child only if your doctor tells you to.
   _____

**TALK TOPICS**

A. What are over-the-counter medicines?
   How are they different from prescription medicines?
   Should you always use over-the-counter medicines?

B. Why are warnings put on the labels of medicines?

C. What do you think a poison control center is?

D. Why should you keep medicines away from children?

**READ THESE DIRECTIONS ON MEDICINE LABELS.**
Talk about what they mean.

A. Dosage: 2 tablets with water every 4 hours, as needed. Do not exceed 10 tablets daily. For children 6–12, half the adult dosage.

1. How many pills can you take at one time?

2. How many pills can you give to a 10-year-old at one time?

B. Directions: for adults and children 6 years of age and older: with head upright, spray 2 or 3 times into each nostril twice daily— morning and evening. Not recommended for children under six.

1. How many times a day can this medicine be used?

2. How much can a 5-year-old use?

C. Dosage: one or two tablets, well chewed, every 2 to 4 hours, between meals and at bedtime. Do not take more than 12 tablets in a 24-hour period.

1. What do you do with this medicine before you swallow it?

2. Do you take this medicine with your meals?

D. Directions: dissolve in 2 or 3 ounces of water before taking. Adults: 1 or 2 tablets every 4 hours as needed. Children: one half the adult dosage.

1. What do you do with this medicine before you swallow it?

2. If you took some of this medicine at 8:00, what time could you take it again?

E. Directions for use:
Child dose: 2–6 years-1 tsp.
6–12 years-2 tsp.
Adult dose: 12 years and over-3 tsp.
Repeat every 4 hours as needed.

1. How much of this medicine can you give to an 8-year-old?

2. How much to a 14-year-old?

**LOOK AT THIS MEDICINE CABINET.**
Talk about what each item is for.

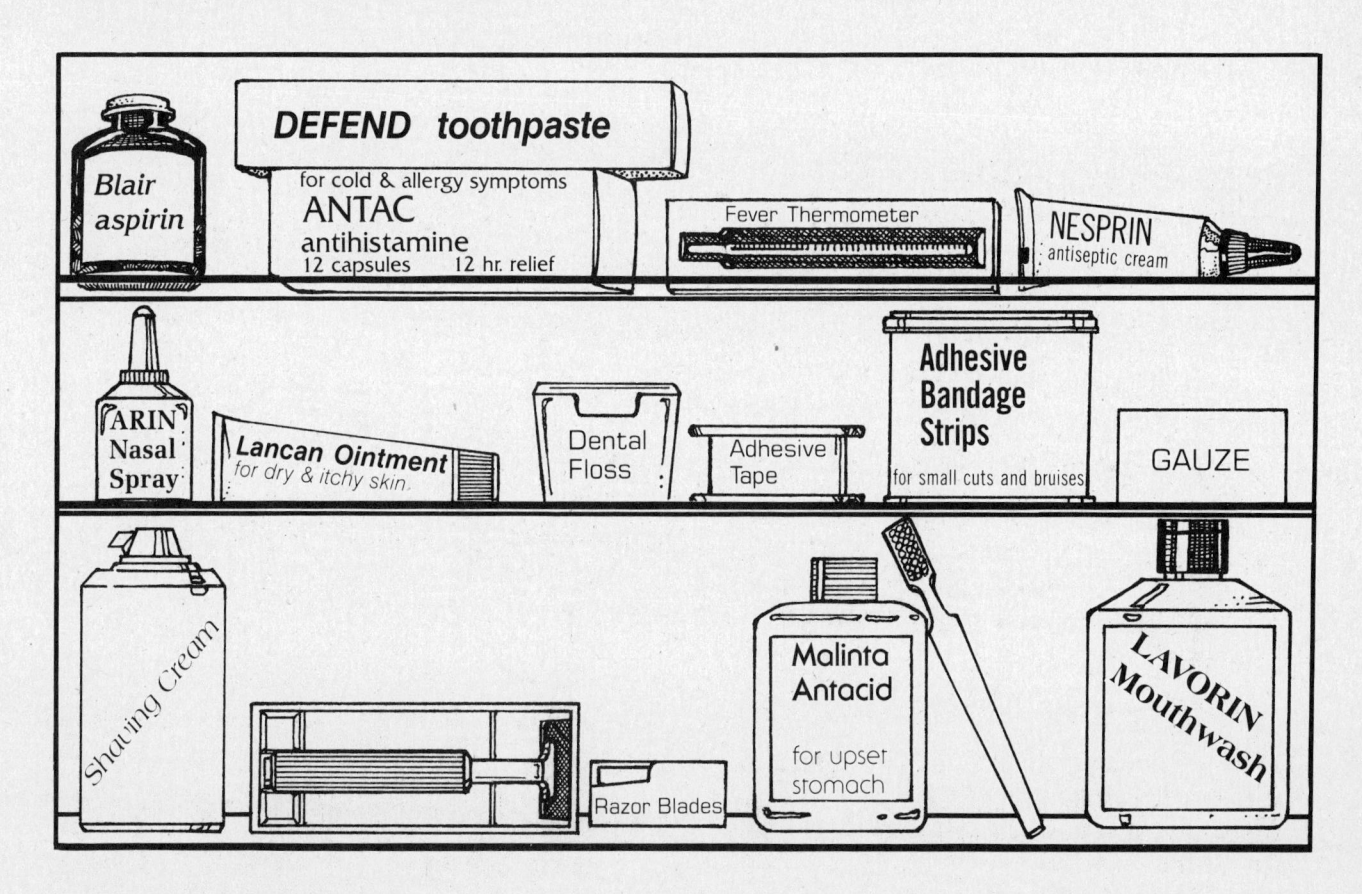

**TALK TO THESE PEOPLE.**
Tell them what they need and where to find it.

PERSON: My stomach is very upset. Do you have anything I can take for it?

YOU: _____ Yes. There's some antacid on the bottom shelf. _____

PERSON: My allergy is acting up. Do you have anything that will stop my sneezing?

YOU: _____

PERSON: I've cut my hand. What should I do?

YOU: _____

PERSON: I think I may have a fever. What should I do?

YOU: _____

PERSON: Do you have any aspirin? I've got a headache.

YOU: _____

83

**READ THESE HINTS.**
**Talk about them in class.**

## HINTS FOR MEDICINE USE

1. Take your medicine as directed—the right amount at the right time.

2. Take the medicine for the prescribed time, not just until you're feeling better.

3. Don't take more than the recommended dosage. If a little is good, a lot is not better.

4. Tell your doctor what prescription and over-the-counter medicines you are now taking.

5. Call your doctor if you feel anything unusual while taking the medicine.

6. Don't take medicines prescribed for other people.

7. Throw away medicines after the expiration date marked on the container.

8. Don't be caught without the medicine you need. Refill your prescriptions before you run out.

**WHAT ARE THESE PEOPLE DOING?**
**Which hint are they following?**
**Write the number of the hint on the line.**

_____ I can't take that medicine. It's prescribed for you.

_____ Doctor, I've been feeling dizzy since I started taking that medicine you prescribed.

_____ Could you refill this prescription for me? I'm almost out of pills.

_____ This label says, "Good until 12/81." I'd better throw it out.

_____ You took your medicine just an hour ago. You can't take any more for three hours.

_____ I feel a lot better, but the doctor told me to take this medicine for 2 more days. I think I'll call him to check.

**TALK TO THIS PERSON.**
He has a headache. Suggest that he take this medicine.

---

**SAYER ASPIRIN**

ADULT DOSE: 1 or 2 tablets with water every 4 hours, as necessary, up to 12 tablets a day.
CHILD DOSE: half the adult dosage. For children under 2 years of age, consult your physician.
WARNING: Keep this and all medicines out of children's reach. In case of accidental overdose, contact a physician at once.
EXP. DATE 7/86

---

PERSON: I have a headache. What should I take for it?
YOU: _____

PERSON: How much should I take?
YOU: _____

PERSON: How often can I take them?
YOU: _____

PERSON: Sounds OK. What should I be careful of?
YOU: _____

PERSON: Is the aspirin still good?
YOU: _____

PERSON: Thanks for the advice.


**TRY IT IN CLASS.**
Your friend has a burned finger. Suggest using this medicine.
Tell how to use it. Tell about any warnings.

---

**CORTAN CREAM**

For temporary relief of minor skin irritations, itching, and rashes due to minor burns, insect bites, poison ivy, soaps.
DIRECTIONS: For adults and children 2 years of age and older— apply to affected area not more than 3–4 times daily.
WARNINGS: For external use only. Avoid contact with eyes. If condition worsens or if symptoms persist for more than 7 days, discontinue use of this product and call physician. Keep this and all drugs out of the reach of children.

**LISTEN TO THESE PEOPLE.**
**They are suggesting treatments that work without medicine.**

I've got a bad headache. Do you have any aspirin?

Why don't you lie down and relax?

Do you think that will help?

That's what I usually do when I have a headache.

---

My nose is all stuffy. I think I'll get some nasal spray.

How about taking a hot shower instead?

Will that clear my stuffy nose?

It works when my nose is stuffy.

---

I need some throat lozenges. I have a very sore throat.

Take some honey. That should ease your sore throat.

Honey? Is that what you take?

Yes. It works well for me.

---

I think I need some sleeping pills. I just can't get to sleep.

Why don't you drink some warm milk instead?

Is that good for insomnia?

Yes. It really helps. Try it. It's better than taking pills.

**FILL IN THE MISSING WORDS.**
**Practice suggesting treatments that work without medicine.**

A. My muscles _____ very _____ . Do you have _____ Deep Rub I can use?

_____ don't you take a hot bath instead?

Do you _____ that will _____ ?

_____ what I usually do _____ I have sore muscles.

B. The baby _____ a stomachache. Do you _____ I should give her some medicine?

No. Give her some ginger ale _____ .

Is that _____ for an upset _____ ?

Yes. It's _____ than giving the baby medicine.

C. I've been having trouble sleeping. I think I need some _____ pills.

How _____ drinking some _____ milk before going to bed?

Is _____ what you do if you can't _____ ?

Yes. It _____ well for me.

**TRY IT IN CLASS.**
**Practice with another student.**
**Look at this list of physical problems.**
**Talk about treatments you can use that work without medicine.**

| | |
|---|---|
| headache | small cuts |
| insomnia | insect bites |
| stomachache | sunburn |
| cold | |

Here's an example to get you started:

YOU: _____Do you have any aspirin? My arm is so sore!_____ (sore arm)
PERSON: _____Let me rub it for you. I'm sure you'll feel better soon._____

87

# CLOSE-UP ON LANGUAGE

## Using question words in sentences

Who, what, where, when, which, how, and why are question words.
These words are also used in sentences that are not questions:

　　I'll call you when your prescription is ready.
　　Aspirin is what I take for a headache.
　　I can't say which antacid is the best.
　　She doesn't know where the drugstore is.
　　Please show me how to use this bandage.
　　There's a doctor at the clinic who is very nice.
　　He wants to know why you are calling.

**FILL IN THE MISSING WORDS.**
Use one of the question words: who, what, where, when, which, how, or why.

A. I don't know __how__ to spell the doctor's name.

B. She takes honey _____ she has a sore throat.

C. I want to know _____ you think.

D. He is the man _____ helped me find the drugstore.

E. They couldn't decide _____ vitamins to get.

F. We found a drugstore _____ the prices are low.

G. I don't know _____ to do about this itching.

H. I don't know _____ you are afraid of dentists.

I. You can go back to work _____ you feel better.

J. I didn't know _____ to stop the bleeding.

K. She asked the pharmacist _____ to use for sore muscles.

L. The doctor told me _____ brand is the best.

M. I showed the doctor _____ the pain was.

N. It's hard to find a doctor _____ makes house calls.

O. I don't know _____ I put the thermometer.

P. She's the druggist _____ helped me.

Q. Put this medicine in a place _____ a child can't find it.

R. Tran asked me _____ I haven't been in class for two weeks.

S. I need to talk to you _____ you have time.

88

## Talking about what someone has asked or said

You can use a <u>direct</u> <u>quotation</u> to tell exactly what someone said:

    Jim said, "Please close the window, Ray."

You can also use an <u>indirect</u> <u>quotation</u> to talk about what someone said:

    Jim asked Ray to close the window.

Read these examples:
    The doctor said, "Take three tablets a day."  (direct quotation)
    The doctor said to take three tablets a day.  (indirect quotation)
    The doctor said that I should take three tablets a day.  (indirect quotation)

    I asked Mary, "Would you drive me to the hospital?"  (direct quotation)
    I asked Mary to drive me to the hospital.  (indirect quotation)


**READ THESE <u>DIRECT</u> QUOTATIONS.**
**Write <u>indirect</u> <u>quotations</u>.**

**A.** She said to the pharmacist, "Please fill this prescription."
                She asked the pharmacist to fill the prescription.

**B.** The doctor said to me, "You're allergic to many kinds of plants."

**C.** The directions say, "Take two teaspoonfuls three times a day."

**D.** The label says, "Keep this medicine out of the reach of children."

**E.** Tom said, "Be careful, Nancy."

**F.** I asked the pharmacist, "Can you recommend something for a cough?"

**G.** Sara said to me, "Take a hot bath for those sore muscles."

**H.** The pharmacist said, "Lancan is very good for itchy skin."

## Using to and for

When you are talking about a reason or a purpose, use to in front of a verb and for in front of a noun:

> I asked the pharmacist to fill my prescription.
> I asked the pharmacist for aspirins.
> She called to speak to the doctor.
> She called for an appointment.
> Take some aspirin to ease the pain.
> Take some aspirin for your headache.

**FILL IN THE MISSING WORDS.**
Use to and for.

A. Come back ___for___ your medicine in a half hour.

B. I'm waiting _____ see the doctor.

C. I'm waiting _____ the nurse.

D. He went to the store _____ aspirin.

E. Jose went to the store _____ buy cough syrup.

F. You can come back _____ see the pharmacist at one o'clock.

G. Lee ran to the drugstore _____ Yung's medicine.

H. Lee ran to the drugstore _____ get Yung's medicine.

I. We called _____ find out about the doctor's office hours.

J. They called the office _____ some information.

K. Can you recommend something _____ a stuffy nose?

L. Can you recommend something _____ take for a cold?

## This, that, these, and those

This and these are used to talk about a thing or things near the person who is talking:

> This prescription is for some antibiotics.
> These vitamins have everything you need.

That and those are used to talk about a thing or things that are not near the person who is talking:

> You'll find the bandages on that shelf near the door.
> Those bandages are the biggest ones we have.

**FILL IN THE MISSING WORDS.**
Use this, that, these, or those.
Sometimes you can use more than one of these words.
Talk about why you used the word you chose.

A. __That__ store across the street is the drugstore I go to.
B. Would you like to buy _____ brand or that one?
C. These aspirins are cheaper than _____ .
D. Take _____ prescription to the drugstore.
E. Can you tell me what _____ words mean?
F. Are _____ vitamins in the window on sale?
G. How are _____ extra strength aspirins?
H. I don't think you need anything stronger than _____ aspirins.
I. The line at this cashier is shorter than the line at _____ one.
J. Where did you get _____ big bruise on your ankle?
K. You can take _____ bottles to the cashier to pay for them.
L. I'd like to return _____ thermometer. It doesn't work.

## Prepositions

At, in, for, on, to, with, about, and between are prepositions.
Notice how they are used:

What did you get at the store?
Don't get it in your eye.
Take this medicine for three days.
Take this to the drugstore.

Take this with some water.
What can I do about this pain?
The directions are on the label.
I can't choose between these two.

**FILL IN THE MISSING WORDS.**
Use at, in, for, on, to, with, about, or between.

A. You have an infection __in__ your chest.
B. You'll have to stay _____ bed for a few days.
C. Take this _____ your meals.
D. You're allergic _____ many kinds of plants.
E. This will help _____ your dry skin.
F. Can you tell me something _____ this medicine?

G.  The pharmacist will find the prescription _____ you.
H.  It's been ready _____ a while.
I.  It'll be ready _____ a little while.
J.  Can you recommend something _____ a sore throat?
K.  What's the difference _____ this one and that one?
L.  I can't choose _____ the name brand and the store brand.
M.  How many pills can you take _____ one time?
N.  Honey is very good _____ a sore throat.
O.  I don't know what to do _____ this itching.
P.  Don't take medicine _____ an empty stomach.
Q.  This prescription is _____ penicillin.
R.  Take one tablet _____ the morning.
S.  Take one _____ bedtime, too.
T.  You might fall asleep _____ the wheel.

## Conjunctions

While, since, before, after, and if are often used to connect two parts of a sentence:

>You must stay awake while you are driving.
>I've been feeling better since I started taking this medicine.
>Take a pill before you go to sleep.
>I'll call you after I see the doctor.
>Stop taking this medicine if you feel dizzy.

**FILL IN THESE MISSING WORDS.**
**Use one of these conjunctions: while, since, before, after, or if.**
**Talk about why you used the word you chose.**

A.  You should stay in bed __if__ you have a fever.
B.  Go to the drugstore right _____ you leave my office.
C.  He has been sick _____ Saturday.
D.  Don't drive _____ you are taking this medicine.
E.  Read the label _____ you start using a new medicine.
F.  Call the doctor _____ you feel anything unusual.

G. You may get a stomachache _____ you take this on an empty stomach.

H. I'll do some shopping _____ you are filling the prescription.

I. I've been sneezing _____ I went to the park yesterday.

J. They've been coming here _____ they moved into the neighborhood.

K. Put a bandage on the cut _____ you put some antiseptic cream on it.

L. You can give this to a small child _____ your doctor says it's all right.

M. Refill your prescription _____ you run out of medicine.

N. My throat felt much better _____ I had some honey.

## Reviewing contractions

Contractions are two words written together, with one or more letters left out. The apostrophe (') shows that some letters are missing. These are some examples:

| | |
|---|---|
| She's got a sore throat. | She has got a sore throat. |
| She's late for work. | She is late for work. |
| You'd better be careful. | You had better be careful. |
| I'd like to lie down. | I would like to lie down. |
| They aren't ready yet. | They are not ready yet. |

**REWRITE THESE SENTENCES.**
**Write the contractions as two words.**

A. You'll have to stay in bed for a few days.

                You will have to stay in bed for a few days.

B. You're allergic to many kinds of flowers and plants.

C. Here's a prescription for some medicine.

D. I'll go to the drugstore as soon as possible.

E. We'd like to see the doctor.

**F.** It's been ready for a while.

**G.** That's the best drugstore in town.

**H.** I can't really say which is the best.

**I.** This one's the kind that I use.

**J.** I've been waiting for a while.

**K.** It's very good for coughs.

**L.** That brand isn't as effective as this brand.

**M.** I'd recommend some warm milk before bedtime.

**N.** What's the matter?

**O.** I'm feeling better today.

**P.** There's a new kind of medicine that will help you.

**Q.** It'll be ready soon.

# PRACTICE ON YOUR OWN

A. Here are some tips on what to keep in your medicine cabinet:

    thermometer—for checking temperature
    aspirin—for fever, headaches, and sore muscles
    adhesive bandages—for small scrapes, cuts, and bruises
    antiseptic cream—for small scrapes, cuts, and bruises
    iodine or peroxide—to clean cuts, scrapes, and bruises
    sterile gauze and tape—for large cuts and scrapes
    scissors—to cut gauze and tape
    tweezers—to remove splinters
    antacid—for upset stomachs
    throat lozenges—for sore throats
    cough syrup—for coughs

Make a list of what is in your medicine cabinet and write down what each thing is for. Look at the directions on all the medicines and make sure that you understand what the labels say.

B. Visit a drugstore. Talk to the pharmacist. Ask him to recommend over-the-counter drugs for: headaches, sore throats, coughs, stuffy noses, itchy skin, and upset stomachs.

C. Talk to friends about treatments that work without medicine. Ask them what they do when they have a headache, sore throat, sore muscles, stuffy nose, or trouble sleeping.

D. Visit several different drugstores. Compare the prices of medicines. Find store brands that are cheaper than the name brands.

# UNIT 4

## THIS IS AN EMERGENCY!

IN THIS UNIT YOU WILL LEARN:

how to report an emergency on the
   telephone
how to describe what the emergency is
how to ask for information about
   a hospital patient
how to understand information given
   in a hospital
how to fill out a form in the
   emergency room
how to give warnings
how to remind people

As you go through this unit,
   notice the following:
**somebody, someone, anybody, anyone,
   everybody, everyone, nobody,**
   and **no one**
**myself, herself, himself, yourself,
   ourselves, themselves, yourselves**
**hold it, stop, watch out, watch it,
   be careful** to give warnings
**remember, don't forget, be sure
   be careful,** and their negative forms
adverbs ending with **ly** (badly,
   carefully, etc.)
adverbs that are the same as
   adjectives (fast, late, etc.)

96

**LOOK AT THE PICTURE.**
Find these things in the picture.

1. ambulance
2. fire engine
3. police car
4. fire escape
5. fire fighter
6. victim
7. stretcher
8. smoke
9. ladder
10. fire hydrant

# TALK TOPICS

**LOOK AT THE PICTURES.**
**Talk about what you see.**

What is happening in these pictures?
What are the fire fighters doing?
What are the police officers doing?
Why was there an ambulance here?
Where did the ambulance take the
    person who was on the stretcher?

Have you ever seen a fire?
Have you ever been in an ambulance?
Have you ever called for an ambulance
    or the fire or police departments?
What other emergencies have you seen?
Have you ever helped someone
    in an emergency?  How did you feel?
    What did you do?

What are some differences between
    this picture and the first one?
Talk about what has changed.

98

**ASK ABOUT OTHER THINGS IN THE PICTURE.**
Use these question words: who, what, where, when, which, how, why.
Write your new words.

11. _____  16. _____
12. _____  17. _____
13. _____  18. _____
14. _____  19. _____
15. _____  20. _____

# REPORTING AN EMERGENCY

**LISTEN TO THESE PEOPLE.**
**They are calling to report an emergency.**
**Notice the tenses of the verbs.**

Community ambulance. Can I help you?

This is an emergency! I need an ambulance!

What is the emergency?

My husband's having a heart attack!

What's the address?

438 Porter Avenue. Apartment 3G.

What's your name and phone number?

Mary Nolan. 324-7841. Please hurry.

An ambulance is on the way. Stay with the victim. Try to keep him warm.

---

Police operator 286.

I want to report an accident. A woman has been hit by a car.

How badly has she been hurt?

I'm not sure. But she's unconscious. Hurry!

I'll send an ambulance. Where did it happen?

On the corner of Broad and Main.

Try to keep the victim warm. An ambulance will be there soon.

> Fire department. Where's your emergency?
>
> There's a fire in my apartment!
>
> What's the address?
>
> 318 River Road. Second floor. Please hurry. I'm choking on all this smoke.
>
> Get out of the building immediately! The fire department is on the way.

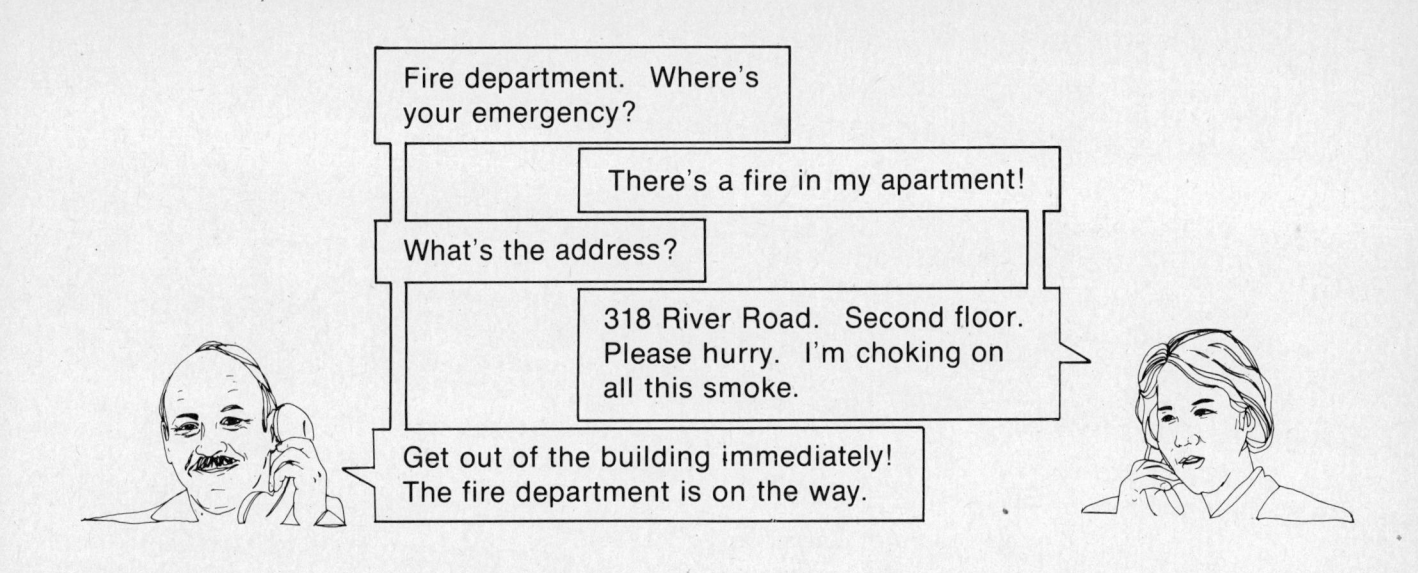

**FILL IN THE MISSING WORDS.**
**Practice calling to report an emergency.**
**Fill in the correct form of the verb.**

**A.**   Community ambulance. Can I __help__ you? (*to help*)

   This is an emergency! I _____ an ambulance! (*to need*)

What _____ the emergency? (*to be*)

   There _____ an auto accident. (*to be*)

   The driver _____ very badly. (*to bleed*)

What _____ the address? (*to be*)

   235 Front Street. Please _____ ! (*to hurry*)

An ambulance _____ there in a few minutes. (*to be*)

**B.**   This is an emergency! There _____ a fire in my house! (*to be*)

   I _____ the fire department. What's the address? (*to send*)

24 Bank Place. Please hurry! I _____ on the smoke! (*to choke*)

   _____ out of the house immediately! (*to get*)

**C.**   Police operator 302. Where _____ your emergency? (*to be*)

   25 Old Mill Road. My father _____ a heart attack. (*to have*)

An ambulance _____ there in a few minutes. (*to be*)

Try _____ him warm. (*to keep*)

**TRY IT IN CLASS.**
**Use the dialogues as examples. Report an emergency.**

**LISTEN TO THESE PEOPLE.**
They are reporting different kinds of emergencies.
Notice how these words are used: **someone**, **somebody**,
**anyone**, **anybody**, **everybody**, **everyone**, **nobody**, **no one**.

---

Hello. This is an emergency!

Please state your emergency.

Someone has cut himself. He's bleeding very badly.

---

Hello. I want to report an auto accident.

Has anyone been hurt?

Yes. Somebody's been hit by a car!

---

Hello. I need an ambulance!

Can you tell me the problem?

Someone's been burned. She's in a lot of pain.

---

Hello. Get me the fire department!

What is the location of the fire?

In the warehouse on Main and 10th.

Has anybody been hurt?

No. No one is hurt.

Is everyone out of the building?

Yes. Everybody's outside.

> Hello. This is an emergency! Get me an ambulance!
>
> Please tell me what happened.
>
> Someone is choking on a bone! Nobody knows how to help him.

---

> Poison Control Center.
>
> My daughter swallowed some bleach! Can somebody help me?

**FILL IN THE MISSING WORDS.**
**Practice talking about emergencies.**

A. Hello. This _____ an emergency!

What _____ the emergency?

There's _____ an auto accident.

Has _____ been hurt?

Yes. _____ is bleeding badly.

B. Hello. _____ me an ambulance!

_____ you tell me the problem?

_____ is in a lot of pain.

I think her leg _____ broken.

C. Hello. I want to _____ a fire.

Where _____ the fire?

The address _____ 211 West Street.

Is _____ out of the building?

Yes. There's no _____ here but me.

D. Poison Control Center.

_____ I help you?

My son _____ a bottle of aspirins.

What should I _____ ?

E. Operator? I _____ an ambulance.

Please _____ me what happened.

Somebody's _____ on some food!

He _____ breathe.

F. _____ me the fire department!

Where _____ the fire?

In the school on Hillside Road.

_____ anyone _____ hurt?

No. _____ is hurt.

Get _____ out of the school.

Everyone's out already.

G. Hello. I _____ to report an accident.

_____ you tell me the problem?

_____ fell down a flight of stairs.

_____ he conscious?

No. _____ unconscious.

103

**READ THESE DIRECTIONS.**
**Talk about them in class.**

---

### EMERGENCY TELEPHONE DIRECTIONS

1. If the victim is injured but breathing, phone for help immediately.

2. If the victim is not breathing, help first and phone later, or get someone else to phone.

3. Call the operator (dial "0") or emergency number (911 in many places), and give this information:

    A. The victim's condition—burned, unconscious, bleeding, poisoned, or other problem.
    B. The address or directions for getting to the victim.
    C. Your name.
    D. The phone number from the phone you are using.

4. Don't hang up! Let the emergency person end the call. There may be questions for you to answer. They may give information about what to do to help the victim until the emergency help gets there.

---

**LOOK AT THESE EMERGENCY HINTS.**
**They tell you what to do in some emergency situations.**
**Fill in the last column with the number you call in your area.**

| SITUATION | WHAT TO DO | WHO TO CALL |
|---|---|---|
| You smell smoke. | Get out of the house quickly. | _____ |
| A room is filled with smoke. | Stay low, crawl along floor. | _____ |
| Someone's clothes are on fire. | Roll the person back and forth on the floor. | _____ |
| Someone is bleeding. | Cover the area and press firmly. | _____ |
| Someone is choking. | Hit the person between the shoulder blades. | _____ |
| Someone has a minor burn. | Run cold water on it. | _____ |
| Someone has swallowed poison. | Follow emergency directions on the poison container. | _____ |
| Someone has stopped breathing. | Give mouth-to-mouth breathing if you know how. | _____ |

**TRY IT IN CLASS.**
Practice with another person.
One person is the emergency operator.
The other person is calling about an emergency.

A. PERSON: _____ (ambulance)
   OPERATOR: _____ (ask about problem)
   PERSON: _____ (heart attack)
   OPERATOR: _____ (keep warm)

B. PERSON: _____ (fire department)
   OPERATOR: _____ (ask for address)
   PERSON: _____ (address)
   OPERATOR: _____ (everyone out)

C. PERSON: _____ (ambulance)
   OPERATOR: _____ (ask about problem)
   PERSON: _____ (bleeding)
   OPERATOR: _____ (cover and press)

D. PERSON: _____ (Poison Control Center)
   OPERATOR: _____ (ask about problem)
   PERSON: _____ (drank cleaning fluid)
   OPERATOR: _____ (follow container directions)

E. PERSON: _____ (ambulance)
   OPERATOR: _____ (ask for address)
   PERSON: _____ (address)
   OPERATOR: _____ (ask about problem)
   PERSON: _____ (choking)
   OPERATOR: _____ (hit between shoulder blades)

F. PERSON: _____ (police)
   OPERATOR: _____ (ask about problem)
   PERSON: _____ (car accident)
   OPERATOR: _____ (ask for address)

# GIVING INFORMATION AT THE HOSPITAL

**LISTEN TO THESE PEOPLE.**
They are in the emergency room of a hospital.

Are you the patient's mother?

Yes. Is she going to be all right?

They're doing everything they can for her. Can you tell me what happened?

She swallowed some pills.

Did you bring the bottle with you?

Yes. Here it is.

---

Are you related to the victim?

No. I'm just a friend.

Were you with him when he hurt himself?

Yes. He burned himself when he was lighting the oven.

Did you put anything on the burns?

No. I just rolled him on the floor to put out the flames on his clothes.

---

What is your relationship to the patient?

I'm her husband. Will she be all right?

Don't worry. She's getting the best care possible. Please fill out this form. Do you have any hospitalization insurance?

Yes. Here's my insurance card.

**TRY IT IN CLASS.**
Practice answering questions in an emergency room.
One person has brought an accident victim to the hospital.
The other person is the receptionist in the emergency room.

A.  RECEPTIONIST: _____ (relative)
    PERSON: _____ (father)
    RECEPTIONIST: _____ (cause of injury)
    PERSON: _____ (fell off ladder)
    RECEPTIONIST: _____ (insurance)
    PERSON: _____ (card)

B.  RECEPTIONIST: _____ (relative)
    PERSON: _____ (wife)
    RECEPTIONIST: _____ (cause of problem)
    PERSON: _____ (heart attack)

Continue your practice. Talk about other relatives, causes of injury, and types of insurance.

**FILL OUT THIS FORM.**
It is from a hospital emergency room.
Fill in information about yourself.

---

**EMERGENCY MEDICAL INFORMATION**

Name of patient _____  Date of birth _____

Address _____

Telephone _____  Marital status  __ single    __ married
                                                  __ widowed   __ divorced

Hospitalization insurance:  Company name _____
                            Policy number _____

Is the patient under medical care? _____  Doctor's name _____

Is the patient taking medication? _____  What kind? _____

Is the patient allergic to any medication? _____  Which? _____

Does the patient have any medical problems? _____

Please describe: _____
_____

---

107

# ADMISSION TO THE HOSPITAL

**LISTEN TO THESE PEOPLE.**
**The doctors are talking about keeping patients in the hospital.**

- We admitted your husband this morning. He's been taken to the intensive care unit.
- How long will he have to be in the hospital?
- I can't be sure. He'll be in intensive care for at least a week. When he is stronger, he'll be moved to a semi-private room.

---

- Your son has appendicitis. We need to get him into the operating room immediately.
- Will he be all right?
- Of course. It's a routine operation. But we need you to sign this permission form.
- OK. How long will the operation take?
- About an hour. You can wait in the waiting room.
- Will I be able to see him?
- You can see him as soon as he comes out of the recovery room.

---

- Your sister has to be taken to the burn ward. She needs special care.
- How long will she have to stay?
- I can't be sure. We'll have to see how fast she heals.

**TALK TOPICS**

A. What is an intensive care unit? Why would a patient have to be in one?

B. What is an operating room? What kinds of operations do you know about?

C. What is a permission (or release) form? Why do you have to sign one?

D. What is a recovery room?

E. What is a cardiac care unit? A burn unit? What other special care units do you know about?

F. How do you find out when you can visit a patient?

G. What is a ward? What is a semi-private room?


**TRY IT IN CLASS.**
Practice with another student. Use the dialogues on page 108 as examples.
Talk about keeping patients in the hospital.


PERSON: Ask about a patient.
(*friend, mother, father, husband, wife, sister, brother, son, daughter*)

DOCTOR: Tell what patient's problem is.
(*heart attack, appendicitis, severe burns, or other health problem*)

Then tell where patient has been or should be taken.
(*intensive care unit, operating room, or other place in hospital*)

PERSON: Ask how long patient must stay.

DOCTOR: Tell how long or say you aren't sure.

Here's an example to get you started.

PERSON: How is my son? (OR How is my son doing? OR Is my son all right?)

DOCTOR: Your son has been in an auto accident.
He's been taken to the intensive care unit.

PERSON: How long will he have to be in the hospital?

DOCTOR: I can't be sure. We'll have to see how fast he heals.

# TALKING ABOUT A PATIENT'S CONDITION

**LISTEN TO THESE PEOPLE.**
**They are talking about a patient's condition.**

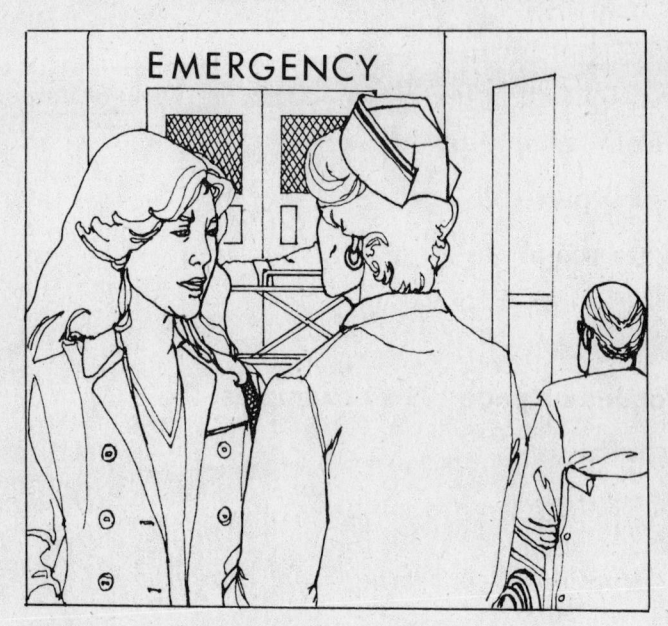

YOKO: How's my sister doing?
NURSE: Her condition is serious, but she should pull through.
YOKO: When can I see her?
NURSE: She's not allowed to have visitors. The doctor is with her right now.
YOKO: Can I speak to the doctor?
NURSE: Certainly. Have a seat in the waiting room. I'll call you when he comes out.

MARY: Is my husband going to be all right?
DOCTOR: Yes, his condition is stable now. He'll be fine.
MARY: When can he go home?
DOCTOR: Not for a while. But he'll be up and around in a few days.
MARY: That's great. Can I see him now?
DOCTOR: Of course. He's in the ward at the end of the hall.

OSCAR: Where can I find Alfredo Castro?
NURSE: I'm sorry. Mr. Castro is not allowed to have visitors.
OSCAR: Why not?
NURSE: Doctor's orders. He's in critical condition.
OSCAR: Critical condition? What happened? He was fine yesterday.
NURSE: Are you a relative?
OCSAR: No. Why?
NURSE: I'm sorry, but I can't discuss his condition. If you'd like to speak to his doctor, I can give you his name.
OSCAR: Thank you. I'd appreciate that.

**FILL IN THE MISSING WORDS.**
Practice talking about a patient's condition.

A. _____ my brother doing?

   His _____ is stable now. He's much better.

   _____ can I see him?

   He's not _____ to have _____ right now.

B. Is my mother going to be all _____ ?

   Yes. She'll be _____ .

   Can I _____ her now?

   Of _____ you can. She's in room 308.

C. When can my father go _____ ?

   Not for a _____ . His _____ is serious.

   What _____ ? He was _____ yesterday.

   I'm _____ . I can't _____ his condition.

   Can I _____ to the doctor?

   Certainly. Have a _____ in the waiting room.

D. Is my daughter going to pull _____ ?

   Certainly. _____ be just fine.

   _____ I see her?

   Not for a _____ yet. The doctor is still _____ her.

E. _____ can I find Peter Lord?

   _____ sorry. He's not _____ to have visitors.

   _____ happened? The nurse said he would be up and _____ in a few days.

   If _____ like to speak to _____ doctor, I can give _____ his name.

   I'd _____ that.

**TALK TOPICS**

A. What does "critical condition" mean?
B. What does "serious condition" mean?
C. What does "stable condition" mean?

111

# WARNING PEOPLE ABOUT DANGER

**LISTEN TO THESE PEOPLE.**
They are warning others about dangers.
They want them to act fast.

Be careful! Billy's reaching for your tea!

Thanks. He almost burned himself.

---

Watch out! The grease in that pan is on fire!

What should I do? Throw water on it?

No! Cover it with a lid. Quickly!

---

Watch it! There's a knife on the floor!

Oh! I almost stepped on it! Thanks for warning me.

---

Look out! You're going to trip on that wire.

I didn't see it. I might have really hurt myself.

You'd better get it out of the way so someone doesn't trip over it.

---

Hold it! Don't pour that paint thinner into that juice bottle.

Why not?

Someone might think it's juice and drink it. They could poison themselves.

112

> Stop! Don't touch that electric cord!
>
> Why not?
>
> Your hands are wet. You'll get an electric shock.

**FILL IN THE MISSING WORDS.**
**Practice warning people about dangers.**

A. _____ careful! Anna's reaching _____ that knife!

　　Thanks. She _____ cut herself.

B. Hold _____! _____ touch _____ hot pan.

　　Oh! _____ almost burned myself. Thanks _____ warning me.

C. Stop! _____ plug so many wires into _____ outlet.

　　Why _____?

　　You _____ start a fire.

D. Watch _____! There's a ball _____ that step.

　　I _____ see _____. I almost fell _____ the stairs.

　　You might _____ hurt _____.

E. Look _____! The bread _____ the toaster is _____ fire!

　　What _____ I do? Throw water on _____?

　　_____! Pull the plug!

F. _____ it! You'd better _____ smoke _____ bed.

　　I won't _____ asleep.

　　You never know. You _____ fall asleep and start a fire.

G. _____ out! Your sleeve is _____ fire!

　　Oh! Help! _____ should I do?

　　Get _____ on the floor! Roll back _____ forth!

H. Be _____! You're _____ to trip _____ that wire.

　　Thanks for _____ me. I might _____ really hurt myself.

　　You'd _____ get it _____ of the way.

113

**LOOK AT THESE HOME SAFETY RULES.**
They tell you how to keep your home safe.

**FILL IN THE MISSING WORDS.**
Use <u>always</u> or <u>never</u>. Talk about what would happen if you didn't follow the rules.

A. __Never__ smoke in bed. You might fall asleep. __Always__ put matches and cigarettes out completely.

B. _____ allow children to play with matches.

C. _____ leave hot oil or grease on the stove. _____ keep the pan's cover nearby.

_____ put water on a grease fire. Water might make it worse.

D. _____ keep a fire extinguisher in or near the kitchen.

E. _____ put poisonous substances into food containers.

_____ keep cleaning products and medicines in their original containers.

F. _____ read the labels on medicines and cleaning products.

G. _____ put medicines and cleaning products where children can get at them.

H. _____ plug too many appliances into one outlet.

I. _____ touch an electrical appliance with wet hands.

J. _____ put sharp tools away immediately after using them.

K. _____ keep stairs and areas where people walk clear of objects and wires.

L. _____ put grease on a burn. Grease traps the heat and makes burns worse.

M. _____ keep flammable liquids (like gasoline or paint thinner) in a place where there is a lot of air.

_____ put flammable liquids near heat or flame.

N. _____ leave young children alone.

O. _____ keep emergency numbers near the telephone.

**TALK TO THESE PEOPLE.**
Practice warning them of unsafe situations.
Use words like <u>watch out</u>, <u>hold it</u>, <u>stop</u>, <u>look out</u>.

A. SITUATION: Someone is about to pull an electric wire with wet hands.
   YOU: _____ Hold it! Don't touch that wire! _____

B. SITUATION: Someone is plugging too many appliances into one outlet.
   YOU: _____

C. SITUATION: Someone's clothes are on fire.
   YOU: _____

D. SITUATION: Someone is about to fall over a wire.
   YOU: _____

E. SITUATION: Someone is about to throw water on a grease fire.
   YOU: _____

F. SITUATION: Someone is smoking in bed.
   YOU: _____

G. SITUATION: Someone is leaving a can of gasoline near the stove.
   YOU: _____

H. SITUATION: Someone is about to put butter on a burn.
   YOU: _____

I. SITUATION: Someone is pouring floor wax into a juice bottle.
   YOU: _____

J. SITUATION: Someone's child is reaching for a hot cup of coffee.
   YOU: _____

K. SITUATION: Someone is leaving a sharp knife on the floor.
   YOU: _____

L. SITUATION: Someone is leaving cleaning fluid where a child is playing.
   YOU: _____

# REMINDING PEOPLE ABOUT SAFETY

**LISTEN TO THESE PEOPLE.**
**They are reminding someone about safety.**

Don't forget to change your clothes before you start cooking.

Why should I change them?

Your sleeves are so loose. They might catch on fire. You might burn yourself.

You're right. Thanks for warning me.

---

Remember to put the tools away after you are finished with them.

But I'll need them again tomorrow.

If you leave them out, people might trip on them. They might hurt themselves.

That's true. I didn't think of that.

---

Be sure to buy a new cord for that iron.

Why? The iron still works all right with this one.

A worn cord might start a fire.

---

Be careful not to clean that toaster while it's plugged in.

Why? It's not on. I won't burn myself.

But you might get an electric shock.

I guess you're right. I'd better unplug it.

> Did you remember to put the medicine away after you took it?
>
> I think I did. I'm not sure.
>
> You'd better check. The kids might take the pills and poison themselves.
>
> You think so? I'd better make sure that I didn't leave them out.

**TALK TO THESE PEOPLE.**
**Remind them about safety.**
Use words like <u>don't forget</u>, <u>remember</u>, <u>be sure</u>, and <u>be careful</u>.

A. Remind someone to dry their hands before touching an electrical appliance.
    Be sure to dry your hands before you touch that appliance.

B. Remind someone to turn off the fire under a pan before they leave the kitchen.

C. Remind someone to replace a worn wire so they don't start a fire.

D. Remind someone to unplug an electrical appliance before they clean it.

E. Remind someone to put medicine in a place where their children can't get it.

F. Remind someone to read the directions on a label before they use the cleaning product.

G. Remind someone to put out their cigarette before going to bed.

H. Remind someone to buy a fire extinguisher for their kitchen.

# CLOSE-UP ON LANGUAGE

## Indefinite pronouns

Anybody, anyone, everybody, everyone, nobody, no one, somebody, and someone are indefinite pronouns.
Notice that they always take the same form of the verb as he or she:

> Was anyone hurt?
> Everybody is out of the building.
> Nobody has work to do.
> Someone is waiting for you.

**FILL IN THE MISSING WORDS.**
**Use the correct form of the verb.**

A. Everyone _____ to know about safety rules. (*to need*)

B. I don't think anybody _____ enough money. (*to have*)

C. Someone _____ looking for you. (*to be*)

D. No one _____ to work late tonight. (*to want*)

E. Someone _____ to call for an ambulance. (*to have*)

F. _____ anyone have the Poison Control Center's number? (*to do*)

G. It seems that almost everybody _____ to watch TV. (*to like*)

H. Nobody _____ to him anymore. (*to talk*)

I. I'm looking for somebody who _____ how to type well. (*to know*)

J. Everybody _____ you feel better soon. (*to hope*)

**FILL IN THE MISSING WORDS.**
**Use someone, somebody, anyone, anybody, no one, nobody, everyone, or everybody.**

A. _____ is choking on some food.

B. Has _____ been hurt?

C. Make sure _____ is out of the building.

D. I'm sure there's _____ left inside.

E. Did _____ call for an ambulance?

F. I called the emergency number, but _____ answered.

G. _____ should learn what number to call in an emergency.

H. I think _____ has gone to call the police.

I. Does _____ have a clean handkerchief to put on this cut?

J. _____ should smoke in bed.

K. Tell _____ to stay away from the burning building.

L. _____ is driving him to the hospital right now.

Notice how indefinite pronouns are used:

<u>All of the people</u> were sitting.     <u>Everyone</u> was sitting.
<u>A person</u> got hit by a car.     <u>Someone</u> got hit by a car.
There were <u>no people</u> at the park.     There was <u>nobody</u> at the park.
Are there <u>any patients</u> waiting?     Is there <u>anybody</u> waiting?

**REWRITE THESE SENTENCES.**
**Use indefinite pronouns for the underlined parts.**

A. Have <u>all the students</u> gone home?
       Has everybody gone home?    OR    Has everyone gone home?

B. I saw <u>a person</u> standing in the doorway.

C. I don't know <u>any of the students</u> in my class.

D. <u>None of the passengers</u> were hurt.

E. <u>All of the people</u> in town are talking about that new movie.

F. Do you think <u>any of your friends</u> would like to come?

G. <u>None of them</u> will want to miss this show.

H. There's <u>a person</u> in my office who looks just like you.

119

## Using indefinite pronouns in negative sentences

Usually, nobody (or no one) and anybody (or anyone) are used in negative sentences:

> Nobody is here right now.
> There isn't anyone here right now.

Notice that you cannot say:

> There isn't nobody here right now.
> OR
> Anybody is here right now.

Everyone (or everybody) and someone (or somebody) are used less often in negative sentences:

> I haven't met everyone yet.
> I don't know if somebody has the time to talk to you.

**ANSWER THE QUESTIONS.**
**Start each answer with no.**

A. Is there someone at the door?

    No, there's no one at the door.   OR   No, there isn't anyone at the door.

B. Can everyone see clearly?
___

C. Can somebody work late tonight?
___

D. Has everybody finished?
___

E. Does anybody know how to speak Chinese?
___

F. Does someone know how to stop this bleeding?
___

G. Was anyone hurt?
___

**H.** Do you think someone can help me?
_____

**I.** Does everybody understand this lesson?
_____

**J.** Is there someone who can show me around?
_____

## Reflexive pronouns

<u>Myself</u>, <u>yourself</u>, <u>himself</u>, <u>herself</u>, <u>ourselves</u>, <u>yourselves</u>, and <u>themselves</u> are reflexive pronouns.

The reflexive pronoun must always match the noun or pronoun that is the subject of the sentence:

I burned <u>myself</u>.   We bought new clothes for <u>ourselves</u>.
He hurt <u>himself</u>.   They should take care of <u>themselves</u>.
She cut <u>herself</u>.   You should behave <u>yourselves</u>.
You will hurt <u>yourself</u>.

**FILL IN THE MISSING WORDS.**
**Use reflexive pronouns.**

**A.** Billy almost burned _____ with that hot cup of coffee.

**B.** Make sure to take good care of _____ .

**C.** Yoko and Kim taught _____ English.

**D.** Lin and I treated _____ to a dinner and a movie.

**E.** You and Jose had better watch _____ when you are using those sharp tools.

**F.** I hurt _____ when I fell down the stairs.

**G.** Sara is going to look for a new apartment for _____ .

**H.** People can hurt _____ if you leave that wire in the way.

**I.** Your kids might poison _____ if they take those pills.

**J.** Clean up after _____ when you're finished painting.

**K.** You could hurt _____ with that knife.

**L.** He bought _____ a new coat.

**FILL IN THE MISSING WORDS.**
**Choose the correct pronoun.**

A. Anna might burn ___herself___ if she touches that pot.   (someone/herself)

B. This medicine might poison _____ if it isn't taken in the right dosage.   (someone/themselves)

C. I'm going to get _____ some new clothes for spring.   (me/myself)

D. Could you give _____ a ride to the station?   (me/myself)

E. Did I hurt _____ with my umbrella?   (you/yourself)

F. Can you make dinner for _____ tonight?   (you/yourself)

G. Give _____ a call tonight.   (her/herself)

H. Tell her to watch _____ when she gets up on that ladder.   (her/herself)

I. Why don't you help _____ to something to drink while I get dinner.   (you/yourselves)

J. Did you enjoy _____ yesterday?   (you/yourselves)

K. Would you tell _____ what is wrong?   (us/ourselves)

L. Could you take a picture of _____?   (us/ourselves)

## Adverbs with ly

Adverbs help describe verbs.
Some adverbs end with ly:

| | |
|---|---|
| badly | I burned myself badly.  (Badly tells how I burned myself) |
| quickly | Get him to the hospital quickly.  (Quickly tells how fast.) |
| carefully | Turn him over carefully.  (Carefully tells how to turn him.) |
| firmly | Press on the cut firmly.  (Firmly tells how to press.) |
| completely | Put out the fire completely.  (Completely tells how much.) |
| slowly | He can only walk slowly.  (Slowly tells how fast.) |

Notice that these adverbs are made by adding ly to adjectives:

| ADJECTIVE | ADVERB |
|---|---|
| bad | badly |
| quick | quickly |
| careful | carefully |
| firm | firmly |
| complete | completely |
| slow | slowly |

**FILL IN THE MISSING WORDS.**
**Use an adjective to describe a noun (a person or thing).**
**Use an adverb to describe a verb (to tell how).**

A. This car is very __slow__ . (slow/slowly)

B. Please drive more __slowly__ . (slow/slowly)

C. Teach your children how to cross streets _____ . (safe/safely)

D. Find a _____ place for all medicines. (safe/safely)

E. You've got a _____ bruise on your leg. (bad/badly)

F. You've cut yourself pretty _____ . (bad/badly)

G. The doctor examined me _____ . (complete/completely)

H. The doctor gave me a _____ examination. (complete/completely)

I. He made a _____ stop when he saw the stop sign. (quick/quickly)

J. He stopped the car _____ when he saw the stop sign. (quick/quickly)

K. Put _____ pressure on the cut. (firm/firmly)

L. Press _____ to stop the bleeding. (firm/firmly)

## Words that can be adjectives or adverbs

Some words are the same when they act as adverbs or adjectives:

| | | |
|---|---|---|
| fast | This car is fast. | (adjective) |
| | Don't drive so fast. | (adverb) |
| hard | That's very hard work. | (adjective) |
| | We are trying hard to finish. | (adverb) |
| early | We ate an early dinner last night. | (adjective) |
| | They started early today. | (adverb) |
| late | He is working on the late shift. | (adjective) |
| | Can you stay out late tonight? | (adverb) |

**PRACTICE USING ADVERBS.**
**Make sentences from these words.**

A. John/bed/early     John goes to bed early.

B. store/open/late    _____

C. mechanic/work/hard _____

D. woman/run/fast     _____

## Using remember, forget, be sure, and be careful in negative sentences

Remember not to smoke in bed.
Do not (don't) forget to watch your kids.
Be sure not to put water on a grease fire.
Be careful not to use grease on a burn.

**REWRITE THESE SENTENCES.**
Start each sentence with remember, don't forget, be sure, or be careful.

A. Don't pour paint thinner into a juice bottle.
    Remember not to pour paint thinner into a juice bottle.

B. Don't plug too many appliances into an outlet.
    _____

C. Read the labels on medicines and cleaning products.
    _____

D. Don't touch an electric cord with wet hands.
    _____

E. Don't let children play with matches.
    _____

F. Put sharp tools away after using them.
    _____

G. Keep emergency numbers near your telephone.
    _____

H. Don't throw water on an electrical fire.
    _____

I. Don't use an appliance that has worn wires.
    _____

# PRACTICE ON YOUR OWN

A. Find out about the Heimlich procedure for treating a choking person. (Many restaurants have a chart that explains this procedure.) Make sure that you understand the directions. Find out what else to do for a choking person.

B. Learn how to give mouth-to-mouth breathing.

C. Find out about first aid and CPR (Cardiopulmonary Resuscitation) classes in your neighborhood. Call up a community health center or high school for this information. If you have time to take these courses, you will know what to do in emergencies.

D. Read labels on the cleaning products and medicines in your home. Make sure that you know what to do if a person swallows the medicine or cleaning product or gets the cleaning product on his body.

E. Find out the emergency telephone numbers for the fire department, police department, ambulance, and poison control center in your area. Be sure to put these telephone numbers near your phone.

F. Think about different ways to get out of your home if there is a fire. Plan some escape routes. Tell your family about these escape routes. Practice getting out of your home quickly, so if there is a fire, your family will know what to do.

G. Find out about smoke detectors. Consider getting one for your home if you don't already have one. If you do have one, make sure that the battery is working.

# UNIT 5

## IS THAT GOOD FOR YOU?

IN THIS UNIT YOU WILL LEARN:

how to talk about diet, nutrition,
   exercise, and stress
how to tell people what you
   can and can't eat
how to make suggestions about food
how to compare exercises and foods
how to talk about what you
   prefer to do
how to talk about how often and
   how long you exercise
how to talk about stress
how to talk about making plans

As you go through this unit,
   notice the following:

questions beginning or ending with a
   negative (**don't you, aren't you,** etc.)
**prefer** or **rather** to show preference

You will also review:

possessives
prepositions with time
comparisons of things that are alike
comparisons of things that are not alike

**LOOK AT THE PICTURE.**
Find these things in the picture.

1. bicycle
2. jogger
3. swimming pool
4. tennis racket
5. jump rope
6. sit-ups
7. drinking fountain
8. ice cream
9. cigarettes
10. fruit

## TALK TOPICS

**Talk about what you see.**

What is this place?
What are the people doing?

What kinds of exercises do you like to do?

What kinds of foods are the people eating?
Are these foods healthy?
What kinds of food do you like to eat?

Which people are relaxing?
What do you do to relax?

What are some differences between this picture and the first?
Talk about what has changed.

**ASK ABOUT OTHER THINGS IN THE PICTURE.**
Use these question words: who, what, where, when, why, which, how.
Write your new words.

11. _____  16. _____
12. _____  17. _____
13. _____  18. _____
14. _____  19. _____
15. _____  20. _____

# STAYING HEALTHY

What do you need to do to stay healthy?
Talk about the following list in class. Do you agree with these statements?

| | |
|---|---|
| <u>Nutrition</u> | Eat a balanced diet. Eat something from each of the four food groups every day. Don't eat foods that contain a lot of sugar or fat. |
| <u>Weight control</u> | Don't take in more calories than you use up. Stay active to keep your weight down. Go on a low-calorie diet if you weigh too much. |
| <u>Exercise</u> | Do some vigorous exercise at least three times a week. Plan to exercise for 30 minutes at a time. |
| <u>Stress</u> | Try to get rid of the stress you feel. Don't make too many changes at once. Express your feelings. Exercise regularly. Plan for fun and relaxation. Get enough sleep. |
| <u>Alcohol, smoking, and drugs</u> | Drink only a little or not at all. Cut down on smoking or stop if possible. And don't take drugs if they are not prescribed by a doctor. |

## TALK TOPICS

A. **Talk about nutrition.** What is a balanced diet? Look at the Basic Food Groups Chart on the next page. Do you agree with this idea of a balanced diet? Do you eat something from each group every day? Talk about what foods you don't eat.

B. **Talk about weight control.** How much do you weigh? Is this a good weight for you? What are calories? How can you find out how many calories are in the foods you eat? What is a low-calorie diet? What other diets have you heard about?

C. **Talk about exercise.** What kind of exercise do you like to do? How often do you exercise? Why is exercise important?

D. **Talk about stress.** What is it? Why do we feel it? In what ways is stress harmful to people?

E. **Talk about alcohol, drugs, and smoking.** How are these habits bad for people? What illnesses are caused by smoking? What illnesses can be caused by alcohol and drugs?

**LOOK AT THIS FOOD CHART.**
**It suggests foods you can eat to have a balanced diet.**

### THE BASIC FOOD GROUPS

| FOOD GROUP | DAILY AMOUNTS |
|---|---|
| 1. **Milk Group**—<br>milk, cheese, yogurt,<br>ice cream, buttermilk,<br>cottage cheese | 2 or more servings daily—<br>1 serving = 1 cup of milk, or<br>1/2 cup cottage cheese, or<br>1 oz. cheese, or 1 cup yogurt |
| 2. **Meat and Protein Group**—<br>beef, lamb, veal, pork,<br>chicken, fish, eggs,<br>dry beans, peas, nuts<br>peanut butter | 2 or more servings daily—<br>1 serving = 3 oz. of cooked<br>meat, poultry, or fish, or<br>2 eggs, or 1 cup of cooked<br>beans or 4 tablespoons of<br>peanut butter |
| 3. **Fruit and Vegetable Group**—<br>all fruits and vegetables,<br>citrus fruits (oranges and<br>grapefruits), fruit juice,<br>potatoes | 4 or more servings daily—<br>1 serving = 1/2 cup of vegetable<br>or fruit, or 1/2 cup of juice.<br>Should include 1 serving of<br>citrus fruit or juice daily, and<br>1 serving of a dark green or deep<br>yellow vegetable at least every<br>other day |
| 4. **Bread and Cereal Group**—<br>bread, dry or cooked<br>cereal, noodles, macaroni,<br>spaghetti, rice | 4 or more servings daily—<br>1 serving = 1 slice of bread, or<br>1/2 cup of cooked cereal, or 1 cup<br>of dry cereal, or 1/2 cup of rice,<br>spaghetti, noodles, or macaroni |

**TALK TO THESE PEOPLE.**
**They are telling you that they don't want a food.**
**Suggest some other food they could have from the same food group.**

PERSON: I don't want any spaghetti, thank you. I don't like it.
YOU: _____How about some rice, then?_____

PERSON: Please don't give me any milk. I don't like milk.
YOU: _____

PERSON: I don't want any orange juice today.
YOU: _____

PERSON: Please don't give me any pork. I don't eat it.
YOU: _____

# TELLING PEOPLE WHAT YOU CAN/CAN'T EAT

**LISTEN TO THESE PEOPLE.**
**They are talking about what they can and can't eat.**

CARLA: Aren't you going to eat breakfast?
RITA: No. I'm on a diet. Haven't you noticed how much weight I've lost?
CARLA: Yes, but isn't it bad to skip breakfast?
RITA: My doctor told me to eat less.
CARLA: He didn't tell you to skip breakfast, did he?
RITA: No, he didn't.

ANGELA: Won't you have some meat?
LEE: No, thank you. I'm a vegetarian. I don't eat meat.
ANGELA: You can't get the protein you need if you don't eat meat, can you?
LEE: Yes. You can eat nuts, dry beans, and peas instead of meat for protein.

SARA: Doesn't your son want some ice cream for dessert?
TERESA: No. He's a diabetic. He's not allowed to eat ice cream.
SARA: He can eat some fruit instead, can't he?
TERESA: Sure. That's a good idea.

ALFREDO: You aren't putting salt on my food, are you?
CARMEN: Don't you like salt?
ALFREDO: I do, but I'm not supposed to use salt. I've got high blood pressure.
CARMEN: Isn't it hard to eat food without salt?
ALFREDO: It was hard at first, but now I'm used to it.

**FILL IN THE MISSING WORDS.**
Practice asking people about their diets.

A. _____ you want a piece of cake?

    No. I'm _____ a diet. I'm not _____ to eat cake.

    _____ it hard to stay on a diet?

    It was hard _____ first, but now I'm _____ to it.

B. _____ you going to have _____ ham?

    No. I only eat kosher food. I don't _____ ham.

You can _____ some chicken instead, _____ you?

    No. This chicken isn't kosher either, _____ it?

No, it _____ .

C. _____ George want any cheese?

    No. He's not _____ to eat cheese. He's allergic

to milk products.

He _____ get the calcium he needs if he doesn't

have milk products, can _____ ?

    Yes. He _____ take calcium pills _____ of eating milk products.

D. _____ you have some wine?

    No, thank you. I _____ drink wine.

    _____ you like wine?

    Yes, _____ I have problems with my liver. I'm

not _____ to have wine.


**TALK TO THESE PEOPLE.**
Ask them questions about their diets.
Start the questions with "Don't you," "Aren't you," or "Won't you."

A.   YOU: _____ (steak)

    PERSON: No. I'm a vegetarian. I don't eat meat.

B.   YOU: _____ (chocolate cake)

    PERSON: No. I'm a diabetic. I'm not allowed to eat food that has sugar in it.

C. YOU: _____ (pork chops)
PERSON: No, thank you. I'm Moslem. I don't eat pork.

D. YOU: _____ (milk)
PERSON: No, thanks. I'm not allowed to drink milk. I'm allergic to it.

E. YOU: _____ (ice cream)
PERSON: No. I'm on a diet. I'm not supposed to eat ice cream.

**TALK TO THESE PEOPLE.**
**They are asking you why you don't eat some foods. Practice telling them that you are not allowed to or not supposed to eat something.**

A. PERSON: Don't you want some cookies?
YOU: <u>I'm on a diet. I'm not supposed to eat cookies.</u> (diet)

B. PERSON: Aren't you going to have a hamburger?
YOU: _____ (vegetarian)

C. PERSON: Won't you have some strawberries?
YOU: _____ (allergic)

D. PERSON: Don't you like ice cream?
YOU: _____ (diabetic)

E. PERSON: Aren't you going to eat some pork chops?
YOU: _____ (Moslem–no pork)

F. PERSON: Won't you have some potato chips?
YOU: _____ (high blood pressure–no salt)

G. PERSON: Wouldn't you like to have some shrimp?
YOU: _____ (heart problems–no shrimp)

H. PERSON: Don't you want some veal cutlets?
YOU: _____ (Hindu–no meat)

**LOOK AT THIS DIET.**
Talk about what is healthy and what is not healthy about it.

THE THREE-DAY DIET—LOSE 10 POUNDS IN 3 DAYS

|  | BREAKFAST | LUNCH | DINNER |
|---|---|---|---|
| Day 1 | 1 grapefruit, 1 slice toast, 2 tablespoons peanut butter, black coffee or tea | 1/3 cup of tuna in water, 1 slice toast, black coffee or tea | 2 slices of turkey, 1 cup of string beans 1/2 cup of beets, 1 small apple, 1/2 cup of vanilla ice cream |
| Day 2 | 1 egg (no butter) 1 slice toast, 1/2 banana, black coffee or tea | 1/2 cup of cottage cheese, 5 unsalted crackers, black coffee or tea | 2 hot dogs, 1 cup of broccoli, 1/2 cup of carrots, 1/2 banana, 1/2 cup of vanilla ice cream |
| Day 3 | 5 unsalted crackers, 1 slice of cheddar cheese, 1 small apple, black coffee or tea | 1 hard boiled egg, 1 slice of toast, black coffee or tea | 1/2 cup of tuna in water 1/2 cup of beets, 1 cup cauliflower, 1/2 canteloupe, 1/2 cup of vanilla ice cream |

**TRY IT IN CLASS.**
One person is on the three-day diet.
You are offering food (using "Don't you," "Aren't you," or "Won't you.")
Use the first conversation as an example.

A. YOU: Aren't you going to have the other half of that banana? (other half of banana)

   PERSON: No. I'm only supposed to eat half a banana. (only 1/2 banana)

B. YOU: _____ (another slice of turkey)

   PERSON: _____ (only 2 slices of turkey)

C. YOU: _____ (another egg)

   PERSON: _____ (only 1 egg)

D. YOU: _____ (some more tuna)

   PERSON: _____ (only 1/2 cup of tuna)

E. YOU: _____ (a larger apple)

   PERSON: _____ (only small apple)

F. YOU: _____ (some milk in coffee)

   PERSON: _____ (only black coffee)

# TALKING ABOUT CALORIES AND WEIGHT

**LISTEN TO THESE PEOPLE.**
They are talking about calories in foods.

- Would you like some ice cream for dessert?
- No thanks. Ice cream has too many calories. I'd rather have some fruit instead.

---

- Please don't give me so much meat.
- Aren't you hungry?
- Yes, but I'm on a diet. I've got to watch my calories.

---

- Would you rather have steak or chicken for dinner?
- I'd rather have chicken. It doesn't have as many calories as steak.
- You aren't on a diet, are you?
- Yes. I'm trying to cut down on calories.

---

- Let's have pizza for dinner, all right?
- Pizza has so many calories! Don't you remember that I'm on a diet?
- Oh yes. I almost forgot. Let's have some fish instead. It hasn't got so many calories.

---

- I'm hungry. What can I eat that doesn't have too many calories?
- How about a piece of fruit? Fruit isn't too fattening.

136

**LOOK AT THIS CALORIE CHART.**
It shows how many calories there are in some foods.

| FOOD | AMOUNT | CALORIES | FOOD | AMOUNT | CALORIES |
|---|---|---|---|---|---|
| Milk, whole | 1 cup | 150 | Apple | 1 | 80 |
| Milk, skim | 1 cup | 85 | Banana | 1 | 100 |
| Ice cream | 1 cup | 270 | Orange | 1 | 65 |
| Yogurt, flavored | 8 oz. | 230 | Grapes | 10 | 35 |
| Yogurt, plain | 8 oz. | 150 | Bread | 1 slice | 70 |
| Egg, boiled | 1 | 80 | Oatmeal | 1 cup | 130 |
| Egg, scrambled | 1 | 95 | Corn flakes | 1 cup | 95 |
| Butter | 1 Tbsp. | 100 | Pizza | 1 slice | 145 |
| Mayonnaise | 1 Tbsp. | 100 | Rice, cooked | 1 cup | 180 |
| Cheese, Swiss | 1 oz. | 105 | Noodles, cooked | 1 cup | 200 |
| Cheese, cottage | 1 cup | 220 | Beans, lima | 1 cup | 170 |
| Chicken, broiled | 6 oz. | 240 | Beans, green | 1 cup | 35 |
| Hamburger, broiled | 3 oz. | 185 | Carrot, raw | 1 | 30 |
| Steak | 3 oz. | 330 | Peas, cooked | 1 cup | 110 |
| Lamb chop | 3 oz. | 360 | Potato, baked | 1 | 145 |
| Bluefish, baked | 3 oz. | 135 | Spinach, chopped | 1 cup | 45 |

**TRY IT IN CLASS.**
**Practice with another student.**
**One person offers a choice between two foods from the chart.**
**The other person chooses the food with fewer calories.**

Offer a choice between:

green beans or lima beans
scrambled eggs or boiled eggs
hamburger or bluefish
skim milk or whole milk
peas or spinach
chicken or a lamb chop

Use these phrases:

I've got to watch my calories
I'm trying to cut down on calories
_____ has too many calories
_____ isn't too fattening
_____ doesn't have so many calories

Use this conversation as an example:

PERSON: Would you rather have green beans or lima beans?
    YOU: I've got to watch my calories. I'd rather have green beans.

PERSON: _____ (offer a choice)

    YOU: _____ (choose food and tell why)

# COMPARING WAYS OF STAYING HEALTHY

**LISTEN TO THESE PEOPLE.**
**They are comparing different ways to stay healthy.**

You're a little overweight. If you want to be healthier, you'll have to lose some weight.

What should I do, Doctor? I've been eating less food.

You need a better diet. And you ought to exercise more.

How will that help?

Exercising burns up calories. The more calories you burn up, the more weight you lose.

---

Let's go for a walk after dinner. We can walk off some of this food.

Let's go bicycling instead. It's more fun than walking.

Yes, but walking is easier.

---

I hate this diet. I'd rather be eating some ice cream.

But this banana has fewer calories. Didn't you say you wanted to take off some weight?

---

I feel stronger since I started exercising.

Really? How often do you exercise?

Twice a week. But I want to do it more often.

138

**FILL IN THE MISSING WORDS.**
**Practice talking about staying healthy.**

A. You need to _____ some weight. You're a little _____.

What _____ I do, Doctor?

You need a better _____. And you need to exercise _____.

_____ will that help?

Exercising _____ up calories.

B. My arms and legs are stronger _____ I started swimming.

Really? How _____ do you swim?

Only twice _____ week. I want to do it _____ often.

C. I need to take _____ some weight. My clothes are tight.

Why don't we go _____ a walk? We can _____ off some of the food.


**FILL IN THE MISSING WORDS.**
**Use comparison words like: more, less, better, fewer, healthier, easier, thinner, and stronger.**

A. The _____ calories you burn up, the _____ weight you lose.
B. The _____ you eat, the _____ weight you gain.
C. Exercising has helped me feel much _____.
D. I weigh _____ since I started swimming.
E. Your heart seems to be much _____ since you started swimming.
F. Walking is much _____, but bicycling is _____ fun.
G. If you want to be _____, you have to exercise _____.
H. If you want to lose weight, you'll have to take in _____ calories.
I. You look much _____ since you've been going to that dance class.
J. You'll feel _____ stress if you get _____ exercise.
K. Since I started exercising I have a lot _____ energy.
L. Fruit is _____ for you than ice cream.
M. My legs are _____ since I started jogging.

# TALKING ABOUT PREFERENCES

**LISTEN TO THESE PEOPLE.**
They are talking about what they'd prefer to (or rather) do.

How about going jogging? It's good exercise.

I really don't like to jog. I'd rather ride a bike instead.

---

I'm glad summer's here. Now I can go swimming.

Swimming's great exercise. But I'd rather play tennis instead.

I like to play tennis too. Maybe we can play together sometime.

---

I've joined an aerobic dance class.

What's that?

It's doing exercise to music. It's fun.

Sounds good, but I prefer gymnastics.

Gymnastics? I've tried that. It was too hard.

---

How about playing a few games of racquetball after work?

I'd prefer to do something outdoors. The weather's so nice.

Would you rather play tennis instead?

Tennis sounds great. I haven't played in months.

**FILL IN THE MISSING WORDS.**
**Practice talking about what you'd rather (or prefer to) do.**

A. How about _____ tennis after work?

   I'd _____ go bicycling instead.

   Bicycling sounds _____ .

B. Would you _____ to play some racquetball?

   _____ rather _____ swimming _____ .

   Oh I love swimming! _____ we can go swimming _____ sometime.

C. How _____ going jogging after work?

   I don't like _____ jog.

   I'd _____ ride a bike instead.

D. I've _____ an exercise class.

   _____ good, but I _____ to exercise at home.

   I _____ to exercise at home, but it was too _____.

   I'd _____ go to an exercise class.

**TRY IT IN CLASS.**
**Practice with another student. One person suggests
an activity. The other person says that he or she would
prefer to (or rather) do something else.
Use the conversation as an example.**

Activities to suggest:

bicycling
swimming
jogging
playing tennis
playing baseball
roller skating
ice skating
walking

Use these phrases:

I'd rather
I'd prefer to
I really don't like to
It's good (great) exercise
_____ sounds great (good)
_____ is too hard

PERSON: Would you like to go bicycling after dinner?
   YOU: Bicycling is great exercise, but I'd rather play tennis instead.

PERSON: _____ (suggest an activity)
   YOU: _____ (say what you'd rather do)

141

# TALKING ABOUT EXERCISING

**LISTEN TO THESE PEOPLE.**
**They are talking about plans.**

I'm getting fat. I can hardly fit into my clothes.

You need some exercise. I was planning to start jogging tonight. How about going with me?

Why jogging? It's not as much fun as tennis.

I know. But jogging uses up more calories.

---

Don't you think we need some exercise?

Yes. I was going to take a walk later.

Well, I was going to ask you to go bicycling.

Bicycling? Walking is so much easier.

Yes, but walking doesn't burn up as many calories as riding a bike. Also, walking isn't as much fun.

---

What are you going to do this weekend?

I'm thinking about playing racquetball. How about you?

I don't know. I was going to do some work at home, but racquetball sounds like fun.

**TALK TO THESE PEOPLE.**
**Practice talking about plans.  Use going to, planning to, or thinking about.**
**Then tell them why you will do something.**

A.  YOU: ___I'm planning to go swimming this weekend.___ (swimming)

  PERSON: Why swimming?  It's not as much fun as playing tennis.

  YOU: ___Yes, but swimming uses more calories.___ (uses more calories)

B.  YOU: _____ (jogging)

  PERSON: Why jogging?  It's not as easy as walking.

  YOU: _____ (better for heart)

C.  YOU: _____ (baseball)

  PERSON: Why baseball?  I thought you liked playing soccer.

  YOU: _____ (more fun)

D.  YOU: _____ (bicycling)

  PERSON: Why bicycling?  It's not as easy as walking.

  YOU: _____ (uses more calories)

**FILL IN THE MISSING WORDS.**
**Practice comparing.  Use as _____ as phrases.  Talk about your answers.**

A.  Walking and playing tennis.   (fun)
  ___Walking isn't as much fun as playing tennis.___

B.  Eating chocolate and eating fruit.   (healthy)
  _____

C.  Walking and riding bikes.   (calories)
  _____

D.  A tennis racket and a baseball bat.   (expensive)
  _____

E.  Soda and milk.   (good)
  _____

F.  Jogging and walking.   (easy)
  _____

# TALKING ABOUT FREQUENCY AND DURATION

**LISTEN TO THESE PEOPLE.**
They are talking about how often they exercise.
They are also talking about how much time they spend exercising.

How often do you go jogging?

Every day.

How much do you jog?

I usually jog a half hour a day.

---

What do you do for exercise?

I go swimming three or four times a week.

How long have you been swimming?

Since I was a child.

---

Do you walk every day?

Yes. I'm up to two miles a day.

I used to walk every day too, but now I hardly ever do.

What do you do for exercise now?

I play tennis once in a while.

---

Don't you ever go bicycling anymore?

Not too often. I hardly ever have the time.

That's too bad. You used to ride a lot, didn't you?

Yes. I used to ride about an hour every day.

**FILL IN THE MISSING WORDS.**
**Practice using duration and frequency words.**

A. What do you do _____ exercise?

    I jog _____ day.

  How _____ do you jog?

    I usually jog an hour a _____ .

B. Don't you _____ play tennis anymore?

    Not too _____ . I hardly _____ have the time.

C. You used to walk to work once in a _____ , didn't you?

    Yes. I _____ to walk every day, but now I

    _____ ever do.

D. How _____ do you roller skate?

    Three or four _____ a week.

    I used to roller skate a lot too, but _____ I

    only go once in a _____ .


**TALK TO THESE PEOPLE.**
They are asking you how often you exercise and for how long. Answer their questions. Use these phrases: every day, once in a while, hardly ever, not too often, ____ times a week, ____ hour(s) a day.

A. PERSON: How often do you swim?
   YOU: _____ Four times a week. _____

B. PERSON: How often do you go bowling?
   YOU: _____
   PERSON: How long do you play?
   YOU: _____

C. PERSON: How often do you go for a walk?
   YOU: _____
   PERSON: How much do you walk?
   YOU: _____

# TALKING ABOUT STRESS

**LISTEN TO THESE PEOPLE.**
**They are talking about feeling stress.**

JOSE: I've been feeling very upset lately.
LAN: What are you upset about?
JOSE: It's so hard to live in a new country and to learn a new language.
LAN: I know how you feel. I've had a hard time too.

TERESA: I keep getting headaches all the time. The doctor tells me I worry too much.
SARA: What's worrying you?
TERESA: My mother is very sick.
SARA: I'm sorry to hear that. I hope things get better soon.

MARY: You haven't eaten a thing. What's wrong?
PETER: I can't eat. My stomach is so upset.
MARY: Is something worrying you?
PETER: Yes. We have so many bills.
MARY: Don't worry. I'm sure we can find a way to work things out.

FRED: I haven't seen too much of you lately.
YOKO: I know. I just don't want to be with anybody. I cry all the time.
FRED: That's too bad. Is there anything I can do to help?
YOKO: I don't think so. But thanks for asking.

# CAUSES OF STRESS

**LOOK AT THIS LIST.**
It shows some problems that cause stress.
Talk about them in class.

1. Death of a husband or wife
2. Divorce
3. Separation from a husband or wife
4. Death of a close family member
5. Injury or illness
6. Marriage
7. Losing a job
8. Pregnancy
9. Getting a new family member
10. Change in how much money a person has
11. Death of a close friend
12. Change to a different type of work
13. Beginning or ending school
14. Change in living conditions
15. Change in personal habits
16. Trouble with the boss
17. Change in work hours or conditions
18. Moving to a new place

**TRY IT IN CLASS.**
Practice with another person. One person asks about the problem and gives sympathy after the other person tells what the problem is.
Use the list of problems at the top of the page.

Use this conversation as an example:

| | | |
|---|---|---|
| PERSON: | What's worrying you? | (ask about problem) |
| YOU: | I'm having trouble with my boss. | (talk about a problem) |
| PERSON: | I hope things get better soon. | (give sympathy) |
| PERSON: | _____ | (ask about problem) |
| YOU: | _____ | (talk about a problem) |
| PERSON: | _____ | (give sympathy) |

## TALK TOPICS

A. Can you think of other things that cause stress?

B. How do people handle problems?

C. Do you think problems can make a person feel sick?

D. Is stress harmful to people?

**LISTEN TO THESE PEOPLE.**
**One person is talking about a problem.**
**The other person is giving advice.**

What's worrying you?

I don't like my job. My boss is giving me a hard time.

Why don't you try to get a new job?

I can't. I don't think I'll find another job that pays as much.

Then try to make the best of it. I'm sure it will get better.

---

What are you upset about?

I got changed to the late shift. Now I hardly ever see my wife.

Don't you see her on the weekends?

Yes, but I'm always tired on the weekends.

Maybe you should look for a new job.

---

What's wrong?

I'm worried about a lot of things. I'm so worried I can't eat or sleep.

You ought to get more exercise. Exercise will help you deal with stress.

---

Is something worrying you?

Yes. School is so hard. I study all the time. I hardly ever sleep.

You really should get more sleep. Then you'll feel better.

# HOW TO DEAL WITH STRESS

**READ THESE SUGGESTIONS.**
They tell you what you can do about stress.

1. If you can, change the situation that is causing the stress.
2. If you can't change the situation, try to make the best of it.
3. Talk to friends and relatives about how you feel.
4. Don't make too many changes in your life at one time.
5. Take time out to have fun and to relax.
6. Get regular exercise. Exercise relieves stress.
7. Make sure that you get enough sleep.

**TRY IT IN CLASS.**
Practice with another person. One person asks about a problem. The second person tells about a problem and the first person gives advice.
Use the suggestions at the top of the page.

Use this conversation as an example:

| | | |
|---|---|---|
| PERSON: | What's the matter? | (ask about problem) |
| YOU: | I just got a new job. | |
| | I'm worried that I won't do well. | (talk about problem) |
| PERSON: | Try to relax. I'm sure you'll do well. | (give advice) |
| PERSON: | _____ | (ask about problem) |
| YOU: | _____ | (talk about a problem) |
| PERSON: | _____ | (give advice) |

## TALK TOPICS

A. What does it mean "to make the best of" a situation?

B. Why should you take time out to relax?

C. Do you think exercise relieves stress? Why?

D. How many hours do you sleep every night? Do you think you sleep enough?

# CLOSE-UP ON LANGUAGE

## Negative questions

Negative questions can begin with the negative forms of:

<u>to be</u>  Isn't this your house?                         <u>Wasn't</u> it a nice day?
        <u>Aren't</u> I thinner than I used to be?    <u>Weren't</u> they happy to see you?

<u>to do</u>  <u>Don't</u> you like wine?                            <u>Didn't</u> they want to go with us?

<u>can</u>    <u>Can't</u> you eat this?                              <u>Couldn't</u> you work less?

<u>will</u>   <u>Won't</u> you eat something?                    <u>Wouldn't</u> you like some cheese?

<u>have</u>  <u>Hasn't</u> he finished yet?                         <u>Haven't</u> they had enough?

**FILL IN THE MISSING WORDS.**
**Practice asking negative questions.**

A. _____ you want to go out for dinner?   (do)

B. _____ you going to have a hamburger?   (be)

C. _____ he want some strawberries?   (do)

D. _____ you like some shrimp?   (will)

E. _____ she eat ham?   (can)

F. _____ you lost a lot of weight?   (have)

G. _____ they left already?   (have)

H. _____ you going to eat anything?   (be)

I. _____ I meeting you at your place?   (be)

J. _____ we have left the blanket in the park?   (can)

K. _____ she coming to the gym with us?   (be)

L. _____ they at the swimming pool last week?   (be)

M. _____ it a warm day yesterday?   (be)

N. _____ you help yourselves?   (will)

O. _____ it been a long time since we went dancing?   (have)

P. _____ you find a better job?   (can)

Q. _____ you get an appointment with the doctor yesterday?   (can)

R. _____ you at home yesterday?   (be)

S. _____ I meet you before?   (do)

## Question tags

Question tags are short questions added to the end of a sentence.
If the sentence is negative, the question tag is affirmative:

He <u>didn't</u> tell you to stop eating, <u>did</u> he?   You <u>won't</u> tell her, <u>will</u> you?

If the sentence is affirmative, the question tag is negative:

You <u>can</u> walk now, <u>can't</u> you?   The fire <u>is</u> out, <u>isn't</u> it?

**FILL IN THE MISSING WORDS.**
**Add tag questions to these sentences.**

A. You've lost a lot of weight, __haven't you__ ?
B. She didn't get hurt, _____ ?
C. Roberto's coming tonight, _____ ?
D. They wouldn't be worried about us, _____ ?
E. Bill doesn't eat meat, _____ ?
F. We can go on Sunday, _____ ?
G. You would rather play tennis, _____ ?
H. I'll see you again soon, _____ ?
I. You aren't thinking about leaving, _____ ?
J. They haven't seen you yet, _____ ?
K. This coat isn't yours, _____ ?
L. He isn't leaving yet, _____ ?
M. They're coming tonight, _____ ?

## Possessives

### Asking about possession

<u>Whose</u> is used to ask about possession:

<u>Whose</u> coat is this?   <u>Whose</u> keys are these?
<u>Whose</u> pen did I borrow?   Can you tell me <u>whose</u> office that is?

### Showing possession

One way of showing possession is to add <u>'s</u> to a noun or a name:

I think that blue coat is <u>Mary's</u>.   The <u>dentist's</u> office is on the left.
The <u>toaster's</u> cord is worn.   The doctor bandaged <u>Jose's</u> knee.

151

You can also add 's to indefinite pronouns to show possession:

Someone's keys were left on my desk.
Everybody's windows were broken.

**PRACTICE ASKING QUESTIONS WITH WHOSE.**
**Answer the question.**

A. (blue car/by fire hydrant)    Whose blue car is that by the fire hydrant?

   (Adolfo)    That's Adolfo's car.

B. (office/on second floor) _____

   (dentist) _____

C. (gloves/under chair) _____

   (teacher) _____

D. (child/next to window) _____

   (Mrs. Brown) _____

E. (windows/open) _____

   (everyone) _____

F. (apartment/unlocked) _____

   (nobody) _____

## Possessive pronouns

Possessive pronouns do not have an apostrophe:

That's my seat.     That seat is mine.
Is this your hat?     Is that hat yours?
Which is her (his) coat?     Which coat is hers (his)?
Our car is green.     The green car is ours.
I think that's their house.     I think that house is theirs.

**REWRITE THESE SENTENCES.**
**Use possessive pronouns.**

A. Is that your blue car?

    Is that blue car yours?

B. My car is the red one.

_____

C. Her bike is next to the tree.
_____

D. Are those our books?
_____

E. His office is the one on the third floor.
_____

F. Their house is the next one on the right.
_____

G. Those are my keys.
_____

H. My car is parked next to your car.
_____

I. That's not their dog, is it?
_____

## Prepositions to talk about time

| | |
|---|---|
| at | Take two tablets at bedtime. |
| on | The doctor has office hours on Tuesdays and Thursdays. |
| in | I'll be with you in a little while. |
| for | I've had this fever for two days. |
| since | He's been waiting since 3 o'clock. |
| from . . . to | We're open from 9 to 3. |
| until | I'll wait for you until midnight. |
| before | I jog every morning before breakfast. |
| after | Do you want to go out after work? |
| during | Don't take more than 8 tablets during a 24-hour period. |

**FILL IN THE MISSING WORDS.**
Use a time preposition.

A. Can you meet me _____ 12 o'clock?

B. If you eat just _____ you exercise, you may get nauseous.

C. I exercise _____ the morning.

D. You should exercise _____ 30 minutes every day.

E. Do you walk to work _____ the winter?

F. Can you come in _____ 8:30 _____ Friday?

G. I didn't fall asleep _____ 2 o'clock.

H. You can come in any time _____ 12 _____ 4.

I. I've been overweight _____ the age of 12.

J. I'm sorry, but the doctor doesn't have office hours _____ 7 P.M.

K. If you want to sleep better, drink some warm milk _____ bedtime.

L. _____ Thursdays, the clinic stays open _____ 8 P.M.

## Making comparisons

To compare two things that are not alike:

Use the comparative form:          OR   Use **not as** _____ **as:**

Jane is prettier than Ann.              Ann is not as pretty as Jane.
Gold is more expensive than silver.     Silver is not as expensive as gold.
Peaches taste better than apples.       Apples do not taste as good as peaches.

**COMPARE EACH PAIR.**

A. Tom is 6 feet tall.    Jim is 6 feet 3 inches tall.
   _____Jim is taller than Tom.   OR   Tom is not as tall as Jim._____ (tall)

B. flavored yogurt–225 calories    plain yogurt–150 calories
   _____ (fattening)

C. Kim walks 2 miles a day.    Carmen walks 3 miles a day.
   _____ (far)

D. Steak costs $3.29 a pound.    Hamburger costs $1.89 a pound.
   _____ (expensive)

E. heartbeat of 90 times a minute    heartbeat of 120 times a minute
   _____ (fast)

F. Ann weighs 120 pounds.    Carla weighs 105 pounds.
   _____ (thin)

G. Lee sleeps 7 hours.    Carmen sleeps 8 hours.
   _____ (long)

To compare two things that are alike, use **as** _____ **as**:

Ann is <u>as old as</u> Jane.
This bottle has <u>as many pills</u> in it as that bottle.
That brand costs <u>as much as</u> this brand.

## PRACTICE COMPARING.
Use **as** _____ **as comparisons**.

A. Tom is 35 years old.    Lee is 35 years old.
   _____Tom is as old as Lee._____

B. The store brand costs $2.98.    The name brand costs $2.98.
   _____

C. a 7½ oz. can of Star Light tuna    a 7½ oz. can of Buzz Bee tuna
   _____

D. Mrs. White's class has 20 students.    Mr. Newman's class has 20 students.
   _____

E. Walking uses 4 calories per minute.    Dancing uses 4 calories per minute.
   _____

F. Angela weighs 125 pounds.    Ann weighs 125 pounds.
   _____

G. Yesterday, Don walked 3 miles.    Today, Don walked 3 miles.
   _____

H. Rick is 6 feet tall.    Mike is 6 feet tall.
   _____

I. Betty earns $250 a week.    Rita earns $250 a week.
   _____

J. 1 Tbsp. of butter – 100 calories    1 Tbsp. of mayonnaise – 100 calories
   _____

K. Rita sleeps 8 hours.    Marta sleeps 8 hours.
   _____

# PRACTICE ON YOUR OWN

A. Look at this chart. It shows how many calories are used in different activities. Compare the activities. Use comparison forms and talk about which activities you prefer.

| ACTIVITY | CALORIES USED EACH MINUTE |
| --- | --- |
| Jogging | 11.0 |
| Swimming | 7.0 |
| Playing tennis | 7.0 |
| Bicycling | 5.5 |
| Walking | 4.0 |
| Dancing | 4.0 |
| Doing housework | 3.5 |
| Cooking | 3.0 |
| Standing | 1.6 |
| Sitting | 1.4 |

B. Make a list of the worries you have. For each worry, think of something you can do to help yourself. Use this example:

| WORRY | WHAT TO DO |
| --- | --- |
| Too much work to do | Ask someone to help you |

C. Find out more about how stress affects people's health. What kinds of illnesses are caused by stress? Find out about ways to relax (like yoga and meditation). Find out how relaxation helps people deal with stress.

D. Ask your friends about the diets they have tried. Make a list of the different diets. Ask your friends how long they stayed on the diets. Ask them if they lost weight. How much did they lose?

E. Use a calorie chart to plan a day's menu. Use the chart on page 137 to help you. Find out how many calories you're supposed to take in for your weight. Make up a menu for that many calories. During the day, write down what you eat. At the end of the day add up your calories. Did you stick to your menu? Did you eat more calories than you were supposed to? Talk about your experiences with a friend or a relative.